Charmed

50 BRACELETS, NECKLACES AND EARRINGS
TO MAKE AND GIVE

Gabriella Sellors

NORTH LIGHT BOOKS

DEDICATION
To my two families, the one I come from and the one I made myself.

Distributed to the trade and art markets in North America by
North Light Books
an imprint of F+W Publications, Inc.
4700 East Galbraith Road
Cincinnati, OH 45236
(800) 289-0963

ISBN-10: 1-58180-897-6
ISBN-13: 978-1-58180-897-1

First published in the United Kingdom in 2006 by
Cico Books, an imprint of Ryland, Peters & Small Ltd
20–21 Jockey's Fields
London WC1R 4BW
Copyright © Cico Books 2006

Text copyright © Gabriella Sellors 2006
Photographs copyright © Cico Books 2006
Illustrations copyright © Cico Books 2006

Editor: Kate Haxell
Designer: David Fordham
Photographer: Tino Tedaldi
Illustrations: Philip Haxell

Printed in Hong Kong

Contents

Introduction

$\mathcal{J}$EWELRY IS PART of human history, as the most ancient archaeological finds have revealed. It can be so many different things: body adornment, a status symbol, a love token, a protective talisman. For each of us jewelry will have, no doubt, a different sort of appeal: for me it is mainly aesthetic and sentimental. We live in a very visual age and jewelry can offer the finishing touch to what we choose to wear and how we present ourselves to the world. I also make pieces of jewelry to mark events in my life and in my family's lives.

The beauty of jewelry-making is that you can make something satisfying at whatever level of expertise you have. And you will never be bored, because there is always something else you can learn. Very little is needed to start at a basic level: a few tools costing less than the price of a good sweater, and a small space—a corner of your kitchen table will do. The techniques shown in this book are easy to follow, but of course, patience is needed for a good result. The points to bear in mind are: never be discouraged and remember that practice makes perfect. So do not be irritated with yourself if your first attempt does not produce a jewelry masterpiece—patience and practice will reward you handsomely!

Charm jewelry is a wonderful field of jewelry-making; you can really let your creativity shine through, and you can make use of so many bits of jewelry with sentimental value, or old pieces that are no longer fashionable. The various colored, semi-precious stones I use have a chromatic appeal that can be very soothing. One basic design can mutate into so many different looks, just by changing a few charms and the stones used. Be warned, once you start making jewelry, you will find it difficult to stop!

Jewelry is one of those skills common to humans of every culture and time and by joining the band of jewelers, you will feel part of this wonderful world. Once you start making beautiful things, you also feel more connected to work of the past, and you will look at museum displays with different eyes and feelings.

I hope you enjoy this book and are inspired to create your own unique pieces of charm jewelry.

LEFT: *A selection of handmade and purchased silver charms used in jewelry in this book.*

GABRIELLA SELLORS

Chapter One

A Charmed Life

Charms in History

Whether we call them by the modern name of "charms," or use the more ancient terms of "amulets" or "talismans," we are talking about the same thing, small, decorative pieces that we believe possess their own powers.

Since before history began people have had a fascination for charms, as archaeological finds in pre-historic settlements show. Shells, such as cowrie shells, have been found in ancient burial sites across the world: the fact that they have been buried with the dead tells us that the shell was held to be important and had powers that continued beyond the grave. Used 20,000 years ago, these shells are

Left: *Keys, symbols of mastery of a new life, are powerful charms for a 21st birthday charm bracelet (see page 34).*

perhaps the oldest known charms, and seem to have been thought to promote fertility and to avert the evil eye.

Nowadays we primarily love charms for their aesthetic appeal, but their origins show that they had a practical purpose. In times when the forces of nature were not explainable, humans needed something concrete to help them feel they were protected from unknown influences, and charms filled that role.

The evil eye concept is present in many cultures and it is always counteracted by specific charms. The scarab, used since 4,000 BC by the Egyptians, is symbolic of the life force, and so protects the wearer against baleful influences. The turtle and the tortoise fulfil a similar role in ancient Eastern cultures.

9

LEFT: *This necklace is made up of traditional ancient Chinese charms symbolizing wealth, wisdom, and eternal love. For example, when you meet your true love, you are supposed to break the jade fish charm into two separate fish and give one to your lover, while keeping the other. As two halves of a single thing, you will always be together.*

BELOW: *As well as representing a birth year in Chinese astrology (see page 16), the snake is a powerfully symbolic animal charm in other cultures.*

With the advent of Christianity, charms became conveyors of faith, such as the charm of St Christopher, protector of travelers. However, the cross symbol predates Christianity by at least 2,500 years and often symbolized protection.

Animal figures were also widely used as charms in the ancient world. Images of falcons, bulls, frogs, fish, and cats were worn as charms to protect and give strength. The snake, used widely in Hellenistic and Roman cultures, had a connection with healing god, Aesclepius.

There is a vast amount of charm history from different cultures to be explored, and we can only touch upon it here. However, if you are interested in this aspect of charm jewelry, a browse on the Internet will turn up a great deal of fascinating information.

The Meanings of Charms

OFTEN YOU WILL use a particular charm in a piece of jewelry simply because you like it. However, many charms do have specific significance, and you can give your piece more meaning by choosing charms that are appropriate to the wearer or an occasion to be celebrated. Different cultures attribute different qualities to various charms, but here are the popular meanings of some of the charms used within this book.

ABOVE: *Heart: the symbol of love and female energy. The Egyptians thought that the heart was the seat of life, soul, and intelligence.*

ABOVE: *Circle: symbol of the ultimate perfect form. For the Egyptians it represented eternity; for Buddhists it symbolizes enlightenment.*

ABOVE: *Flower: different types of flower do carry quite different symbolic meanings, but flowers in general represent natural beauty.*

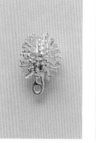

ABOVE: *Fish: offers good luck and keeps you safe from drowning. An early Christian symbol and an ancient Indian symbol— the first incarnation of the god Vishnu was as a fish.*

ABOVE: *Porcupine: this animal often symbolizes a pure innocence.*

ABOVE: *Key: helps in establishing a new life and gives mastery of a situation.*

ABOVE: *Lizard: represents dreaming, foresight, and ancient secrets.*

ABOVE: *Seahorse: this represents confidence, grace, and male energy.*

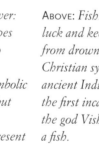

ABOVE: *Spiral: the symbol of death and rebirth—the cycle of life.*

ABOVE: *Star: the five-pointed star had a role in magic. Also a charm for sailors.*

ABOVE: *Starfish: the five arms symbolize the forms of earthly happiness—longevity, wealth, peace, virtue, and happiness.*

❧ The Properties of Semi-precious Stones ❧

LIKE CHARMS, some stones are attributed with particular qualities. Use these stones to imbue your charm jewelry with powers to help the wearer achieve specific goals or avert misfortune. Here are some of the qualities associated with stones used in jewelry in this book.

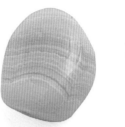

LEFT: *Malachite: absorbs pollutants; guards against radiation; the stone of transformation; encourages positive risk taking.*

LEFT: *Aventurine: calms anger and irritation; aids prosperity and creativity.*

ABOVE: *Agate (blue lace): calming; neutralizes anger and mental stress.*

RIGHT: *Fluorite: dispels electromagnetic stress; good protection against computer stresses.*

LEFT: *Amber: a protective stone; deflects electricity; balances emotions.*

LEFT: *Garnet (red and green): regenerates the body; stimulates the metabolism; an energizing stone.*

LEFT: *Amazonite: dispels worries and fears; has a filtering action to absorb microwave and cell phone emissions.*

LEFT: *Jade: in the East this has had magical and spiritual qualities since ancient times; a symbol of purity and serenity.*

RIGHT: *Kyanite: aids in communication; dispels confusion.*

ABOVE: *Citrine: brings inner calm; aids concentration; overcomes depression.*

LEFT: *Rose quartz: the most important stone for the heart, a stone of unconditional love and peace; calming; an emotional healer.*

LEFT: *Pearl: attracts love; soothes the heart chakra.*

RIGHT: *Rhodonite: a first aid stone—heals emotional shock and panic.*

RIGHT: *Turquoise: a healing stone; protects against pollutants; helps with problem solving; stabilizes mood swings.*

LEFT: *Crysoprase: aids meditation and insight; helps you find positive solutions; very calming.*

RIGHT: *Amethyst: balances the emotions; a very protective stone; promotes love; blocks geopathic stress; a natural tranquilizer.*

Combining Stones & Charms

If YOU MATCH symbolic silver charms with stones whose qualities complement them, you can produce very powerful charms. This can be done either by using a charm shape made from the appropriate stone, by hanging the two pieces together on a jump ring or mixing them in a multi-piece charm (see page 123). You can work out favorable combinations by consulting the charms glossary (see page 11) and stones glossary (see page 12).

ABOVE: *Fish and aquamarine: the symbol and birthstone of Pisces, both are talismans against drowning.*

ABOVE: *Heart and rose quartz: the symbol and stone of love —a powerful combination for mending broken relationships.*

Choosing & Using Different Charm Elements

Making jewelry using a mix of purchased and handmade charms (see pages 110–124) is, to my mind, the most effective choice. You will have the widest range of colors, shapes, and finishes to choose from, and you can produce the most personalized pieces.

When choosing elements for a piece of jewelry, be aware of these different qualities, and of the general effect you are trying to achieve. It is an overall, cohesive design you need to aim for: it is very easy to get caught up in details and forget the whole (as with almost everything in life!)

The weight of the charms plays a part in the finished design as well: a chunky look is great, but can be heavy to wear. A delicate piece may feel lost unless teamed with a simple outfit, but it is very wearable.

LEFT: *A mix of handmade and purchased silver charms with baroque and carved stones can make for an interesting, contemporary piece of jewelry.*

~ *Working with Color* ~

*T*HE MAIN REASON most of us choose a particular color is because we like it and it suits us, and those are very good reasons to have. There are lots of opinions on what shades work well with different skin or hair colors, and it is possible to have your colors "done" to find out which color palette will suit you best. However, there are no hard and fast rules: feel completely free to wear what you like, though I must say that I think all redheads look stunning wearing green stones!

Be bold and experiment with color: try working with different shades in the same color palette, or using a strongly contrasting color to highlight or enhance another color. Look at the many designs in this book and see how the careful balances of colors work to unify different elements.

Colors do have meanings associated with them, and these can be interesting if you want to make a very symbolic piece of jewelry. So many different cultures, faiths, and practices associate different colors with varying occasions, rituals, and symbolic status that it is impossible to list all the meanings on these pages. However, there are various generally accepted thoughts on the influences of some colors, and they are given here.

ABOVE: **PURPLE**

A noble, spiritual color that is sacred in nature: flowers such as violets and orchids are delicate and precious. Mixed from warm red and cool blue, purple—and its associated shades of lilac, mauve, and violet—carries some properties of both original colors. Purple can boost the imagination and help creativity.

ABOVE: **BROWN**

This color covers such a wide spectrum from bright rust to deepest chocolate that it is hard to see why anyone would think it dull, though it is burdened with this reputation. Brown is a natural color and represents simplicity, honesty, warmth and health.

ABOVE: PINK

Feminine, healing, comforting, and affectionate, pink is the ultimate girl color. From the softest pastels found in rose quartz to the hot pinks found in tropical flowers, pink is a natural color that can be used to express the finer feelings.

ABOVE: WHITE AND GRAY

White is sometimes seen as a "non-color" but nothing could be further from the truth. White symbolizes purity, sincerity, and precision. A feminine color, associated with the Moon, it can balance and enhance other colors.

Gray is often thought to be a cold color, but it comes in so many shades from rich browny-gray to steely blue-gray, that it is hard to see how they can all be considered in the same way.

ABOVE: GREEN

The color of life, green symbolizes renewal, growth, and health. Restful and calming, green will soothe mental and physical stress, and convey harmony and stability. Use several shades of green together to create a fresh, springtime feel in a piece of jewelry.

LEFT: AQUA

Mixed from blue and green, the aqua color palette carries wonderful properties from both. Refreshing and calming, aqua is a light, strong color that is associated with peace and an open-hearted approach to the world.

RIGHT: BLUE

Another natural color, whether it be the blue of the sea or the sky. This color can be strong and steadfast, or light and friendly depending on the shade. It is a soothing color and time will seem to pass more quickly under its influence.

The Zodiac

WESTERN ASTROLOGICAL SIGNS first came from Mesopotamia thousands of years ago, and spread to Greece and Egypt. Many constellations had animal names, so the Greeks called them "the circle of animals"; in Greek this is *zoidiakos cyclos*, hence the modern name, Zodiac. The Zodiac chapter in this book (see pages 37–53) has ideas for jewelry featuring specific birthstones, but you can change any of these to suit the wearer of the piece.

JANUARY and CAPRICORN: garnet.
FEBRUARY and AQUARIUS: amethyst.
MARCH and PISCES: aquamarine.
APRIL and ARIES: diamond.
MAY and TAURUS: emerald or crysoprase.
JUNE and GEMINI: pearl.
JULY and CANCER: ruby.
AUGUST and LEO: peridot.
SEPTEMBER and VIRGO: sapphire.
OCTOBER and LIBRA: opal.
NOVEMBER and SCORPIO: citrine.
DECEMBER and SAGITTARIUS: turquoise or lapis lazuli.

THE CHINESE ZODIAC works differently in that the year of your birth is represented by an animal symbol. Each animal has different qualities and these are reflected in your personality and the way in which you face life. There are twelve animals running in a twelve-year cycle, so consult a Chinese almanac to establish which animal presides over the year of your birth. Given here are the animals and some of their primary qualities.

RAT: charming, perfectionist, thrifty, and ambitious.
OX: patient, eccentric, alert, and stubborn.
TIGER: sensitive, short-tempered, indecisive, and courageous.
RABBIT (or Hare): talented, virtuous, gossipy, and wise.
DRAGON: energetic, brave, eccentric, and soft-hearted.
SNAKE: wise, fortunate, selfish, and passionate.
HORSE: popular, good with their hands, impatient, and out-going.
SHEEP (or Ram): elegant, timid, passionate, and gentle.
MONKEY: skillful, inventive, decisive, and strong-willed.
ROOSTER: capable, eccentric, interesting, and brave.
DOG: loyal, honest, stubborn, and good leaders.
PIG: chivalrous, loyal, quick-tempered, and kind.

Reviving Old Jewelry

ABOVE: *Vintage beads are given a new lease of life.*

MAYBE YOU HAVE LOST one of a pair of favorite earrings, broken a necklace, or been given grandma's brooch, minus its pin: what can you do with the pieces? It is easy to create a new piece of jewelry that carries some of the sentimental attachments of the old pieces. Any of these components can be put together to make something personal, imaginative, and meaningful, just by adding chain, a clasp, and maybe a few extra beads. The Oriental-style Bracelet (see left and page 83) is made in this way. Look upon the broken pieces as individual elements, read the section on designing a bracelet (see page 17) and apply the same principles to the piece you want to make.

Designing a Bracelet

THE PRINCIPLES OF ARRANGING different elements and colors are shown here on a bracelet, but they can be applied to any piece of jewelry you are making. Here, the same elements are arranged in three different ways to produce very different results.

If it is a bracelet you are working on, remember that it will be seen in the round when you are wearing it, so the beginning and end must work together as well as the middle section.

When designing a piece of jewelry, do work in this way: lay everything out flat on a table and move the pieces around until you are happy with the arrangement. Only then should you start threading up your stone charms and attaching the pieces to the chain.

If you have a digital camera it is a good idea to take a snap of the final arrangement, then you don't have to worry about remembering exactly what goes where.

ABOVE: *Light pink slowly moves into lilac, and then into dark notes. The silver pieces are contained within the lighter end of the bracelet to highlight the effect. Here there will be an abrupt change of color when the bracelet is fastened, but it will be striking and effective.*

RIGHT: *Darker colors cluster at one end with the light, ethereal silver charms in the middle, moving into soft pink tones at the other end of the bracelet. When the bracelet is fastened the end colors will crash into one another, but as they all work together this will not look odd.*

ABOVE: *Soft lilac tones come crashing into dark colors in the middle of the bracelet. These then wane into soft pink and finally wax into a surprisingly strong purple fluorite stone that will sit happily next to the lilac when the bracelet is fastened. The silver charms are scattered between the stones for overall lightness.*

Chapter Two

Love

ABOVE: *A simple silver necklace with symbols of male and female energy (see page 11).*

Give a gift of charmed love to someone special in your life, whether it be a dear friend, cherished family member, or your one true love. In this chapter you'll find suitable designs for all your loved ones, from pretty feminine pieces for girlfriends, through a simple necklace suitable for a man. There is a beautiful set of earrings and necklace set full of symbolism and love for a new mother, a pretty bracelet to celebrate a milestone birthday, cute gifts for friends and family, and even a gift wrap charm that will find further use as a bag charm once the gift is unwrapped. Whatever design you choose to make, you can be sure your gift of love will be appreciated.

~ Heart Bookmark ~

MATERIALS
8¾ in (22 cm) of 1.5 mm wire
12 in (30 cm) of thin, black
  leather cord
1½ in (4cm) of 0.5 mm wire
1¼ in (3 cm) of 1.2 mm wire
One large and one small sea
  bamboo bead
One flat silver bead

TO MAKE
Working from one end of the 1.5 mm wire, make a heart shape. Bend the remaining straight section of wire down through the middle of the heart, following the photograph. Hammer the heart and texture the straight section with fabric. Make the beads into a multi-piece charm, using the 0.5 mm wire and small sea bamboo bead to make a curly ended lower section, and the 1.2 mm wire and remaining beads for the top section. Fold the leather cord in half and loop it over one side of the heart. Tie an overhand knot 1½ in (4 cm) from the ends, thread on the charm, and tie another knot to hold it in place.

TECHNIQUES
Curly headpin, page 105
Wire heart charm, page 113
Using fabrics, page 119
Hammering, page 120
Multi-piece charm, page 123

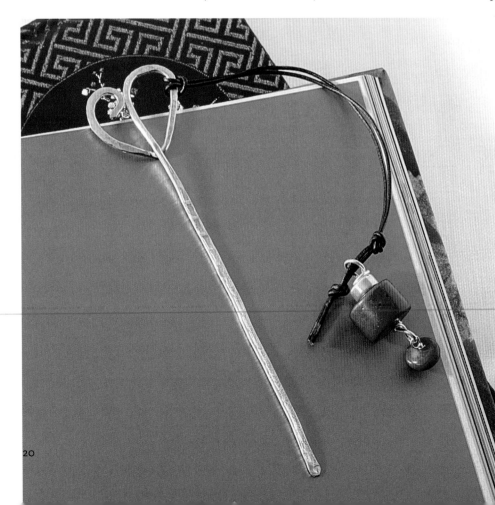

LEFT: A gift of love for a literary friend—a bookmark that will have a permanent place in their heart.

ᆗ Parcel Charm ᆗ

MATERIALS

3¼ in (8 cm) of 1.5 mm wire
1¼ in (3 cm) of fine
 belcher chain
2½ in (6 cm) of 0.5 mm wire
One small and one large
 amethyst heart
One baroque amethyst bead
One purchased silver
 heart charm

TECHNIQUES

Purchased chain, page 100
Hook clasp, page 102
Jump rings, page 104
Curly headpin, page 105
Looped top charm, page 121
Attaching charms directly,
 page 125
Attaching charms and clasps
 with jump rings, page 126

TO MAKE

Make 2¾ in (7 cm) of the 1.5 mm wire into a hook clasp and slip one side of it through one end of the chain. Use the 0.5 mm wire and amethysts to make three looped top charms with curly ends and attach them directly to the chain, following the photograph. Make the remaining 1.5 mm wire into a jump ring and attach the heart charm to the chain with it.

RIGHT: *Make a special birthday present even more amazing by decorating the gift bow with this little charm. Once the present is unwrapped, the charm can be used to adorn an evening bag.*

Charm Anklet

TECHNIQUES.
Purchased chain, page 100
Jump rings, page 104
Curly headpin, page 105
Multi-piece charm, page 123
Attaching charms and clasps
with jump rings, page 126

TO MAKE
Make the 1.5 mm wire into 14 jump rings. Attach the two parts of the clasp to the ends of the chain. Use the 0.5 mm wire and the pearls and stones to make nine multi-piece charms with curly ends, following the photograph. Attach all the charms to the chain with jump rings.

MATERIALS
6 in (15 cm) of 1.5 mm wire
Silver magnetic clasp
10 in (25 cm) of medium
    belcher chain
16 in (40 cm) of 0.5mm wire
Three ½ in (10 mm) rose
    quartz hearts
One ½ in (10 mm) blue lace
    agate heart
Two ¼ in (6 mm) blue lace
    agate hearts
Two ¼ in (6 mm) blue lace
    agate stars
One medium blue
    freshwater pearl
Five small pink
    freshwater pearls
Three small blue
    freshwater pearls
One ⅛ in (4 mm) blue lace
    agate round bead
Purchased lizard, seahorse,
    and starfish charms

ABOVE AND BELOW: *An almost ethereal ankle bracelet, a dancing ensemble of pretty quartz and agate stars and hearts combined with symbolic animal charms. A gift of love and good wishes for the future.*

Earrings with
∽ Jade & Silver Charms ∽

MATERIALS
3½ in (9 cm) of 0.8 mm wire
3 in (8 cm) of 1.5 mm wire
4½ in (11 cm) of small and
    5½ in (14 cm) of very fine
    belcher chain
4 in (10 cm) of 0.5 mm wire
One small jade star and heart
One medium jade star
    and heart
Two purchased butterfly,
    one key and one
    handbag charm

TECHNIQUES
Purchased chain, page 100
Jump rings, page 104
Standard ear wires, page 107
Looped top charm, page 121
Attaching charms directly,
    page 125
Attaching charms and clasps
    with jump rings, page 126

TO MAKE
Make the 0.8 mm wire into two ear wires and the 1.5 mm
wire into eight jump rings. Cut the small chain into two
2¼ in (5.5 cm) lengths, and the very small chain into two
1¾ in (4.5 cm), and two 1 in (2.5 cm) lengths. Thread one of
each length of chain onto one of two jump rings and fasten
one ring to each ear wire. Make the jade stars and hearts
into four looped top charms. Using jump rings, attach the
charms to the ends of the chain and to the ring holding the
chain to the ear wires, following the photograph.

RIGHT: *Very delicate earrings with jade hearts and stars as
charms, as well as a silver key and a butterfly. Jade is thought
to be very protective in the East. The silver key charms make
them suitable as a 21st birthday present.*

Heart Bracelet

MATERIALS
29 in (73 cm) of 1.5 mm wire
One purchased large ring
10 in (25 cm) of
     0.5 mm wire
One blue lace agate bead
One purchased star and one
     heart charm
Three large amethyst hearts
Two large and three small rose
     quartz hearts
Two small blue lace
     agate hearts
4 x ¾ in (10 x 2 cm) of
     sheet silver

TECHNIQUES
Handmade chain, page 98
T-bar clasp, page 103
Jump rings, page 104
Heart charm, page 116
Drilling a charm, page 118
Using fabrics, page 119
Looped top charm, page 121
Multi-piece charm, page 123
Attaching charms directly,
     page 125
Attaching charms and clasps
     with jump rings, page 126

TO MAKE
Make 24 in (60 cm) of 1.5 mm wire into handmade chain. Make 3 in (8 cm) into eight jump rings and 1¾ in (4.5 cm) into a T-bar clasp. Attach the clasp and large ring to the ends of the chain. Use 0.5 mm wire and the round bead to make a looped top charm, then attach it and the star to the large ring. Use 0.5 mm wire to make the stone hearts into five multi-piece charms and attach them directly, following the photograph. Make four heart charms from the sheet silver and texture them. Drill a hole in each heart. Attach the purchased and silver hearts with jump rings, spacing all the charms evenly.

LEFT AND RIGHT: *Strung with silver and pretty pastel-colored hearts made from stones that promote love, this bracelet is the ultimate token of affection for a true friend.*

LOVE

Spiral Necklace & Earrings

NECKLACE MATERIALS
10½ in (27 cm) of 1.5 mm wire
16 in (40 cm) of fine belcher chain
24½ in (62 cm) of 1.2 mm wire
Two ⅝-in (15-mm) and two ½-in (10-mm) discs
8 in (20 cm) of 0.5 mm wire
One small pink, two small blue, and one medium blue freshwater pearl
Two small blue lace agate hearts and one star
One small rose quartz star, heart and oval bead
One rhodonite cube bead

NECKLACE TECHNIQUES
Purchased chain, page 100
Hook clasp, page 102
Jump rings, page 104
Curl charm, page 110
Music note charm, page 115
Disc charm, page 118
Drilling a charm, page 118
Hammering, page 120
Looped top charm, page 121
Multi-piece charm, page 123
Attaching charms and clasps with jump rings, page 126

TO MAKE NECKLACE

Make 2¾ in (7cm) of 1.5 mm wire into a hook clasp and the rest into 18 jump rings. Attach the hook and a ring to the ends of the chain. Make three large curl charms, each from 3½ in (9 cm) of 1.2 mm wire, and four smaller curl, each from 2¾ in (7 cm) of 1.2 mm wire. Make a music note charm from 2¾ in (7 cm) of 1.2 mm wire. Hammer all the curls and the discs to texture them. Drill two opposite holes on the edge of each disc. Use the 0.5 mm wire and stones and pearls to make 11 looped top charms. Make all of the charms, except one small blue and one small pink pearl, into multi-piece charms, following the photograph. Attach the charms to the chain with jump rings, positioning one in the middle and spacing the others evenly either side.

LEFT, ABOVE, AND OPPOSITE: *A stunningly beautiful, as well as symbolic, necklace and earring set to give a new mother to celebrate the baby's birth. The spiral is the sign of the cycle of life and the disc represents eternity, and here they are combined with the love offered by the rose quartz and pearls, and the calmness the agate brings.*

EARRING MATERIALS
3¼ in (8 cm) of 0.8 mm wire
7 in (18 cm) of 1.2 mm wire
14 in (35 cm) of 0.5 mm wire
Two blue lace agate hearts,
    stars, cubes, and
    round beads
Eight blue freshwater pearls

EARRING TECHNIQUES
Simple ear wires, page 106
Curl charm, page 110
Hammering, page 120
Multi-piece charm, page 123

TO MAKE EARRINGS
Make the 0.8 mm wire into
two simple ear wires and the
1.2 mm wire into two
spirals. Hammer the spirals.
Make the stones and pearls
into multi-piece charms,
following the photograph,
and hang them from the
spirals. Hang the spirals
from the ear wires.

MATERIALS

8 in (20 cm) of 1.5 mm wire
Medium trigger clasp
7 in (18 cm) of medium
    belcher chain
7 in (18 cm) of 0.5mm wire
Nine flat sea bamboo beads
Four purchased shoe and five
    bag charms

TECHNIQUES

Purchased chain, page 100
Purchased clasps, page 101
Jump rings, page 104
Looped top charm, page 121
Attaching charms and clasps
    with jump rings, page 126

Handbags & Heels Bracelet

TO MAKE

Make the 1.5 mm wire into 20 jump rings. Attach the clasp and a ring to the ends of the chain. Use the 0.5 mm wire to make the beads into nine looped top charms. Using jump rings and spacing them evenly, attach alternate silver and sea bamboo charms to the chain.

RIGHT: *No lady can have enough shoes and bags, so why not commemorate a friend's love of the finest accessories with this pretty, witty collection of both?*

Pink Charm Brooch

MATERIALS

9½ in (24 cm) of 1.5 mm wire
4¾ in (12 cm) of 0.5 mm wire
One large flat, two cylinder
    and one baroque
    rhodonite bead
One large rose quartz bead
One iridescent freshwater
    pearl stick bead
1¼ in (3 cm) of 1.2 mm wire

TECHNIQUES

Jump rings, page 104
Brooch pin, page 108
Hammered spike charm,
    page 112
Multi-piece charm, page 123
Attaching charms and clasps
    with jump rings, page 126

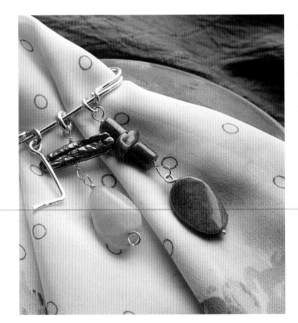

TO MAKE

Make 8 in (20 cm) of 1.5 mm wire into a brooch pin and the remainder into three jump rings. Use the 0.5 mm wire, the beads, and the pearl to make two multi-piece charms, following the photograph. Make a spike charm from the 1.2 mm wire, but do not hammer the end very flat. With chain-nosed pliers, bend the spike ½ in (1 cm) from the end to form an "L" shape. Attach the charms with jump rings.

LEFT: *Pretty in pink: a brooch to charm the most stylish of friends.*

MATERIALS

3 in (8 cm) of 1.5 mm wire
Small trigger clasp
7 in (18 cm) of fine belcher chain
12¼ in (32 cm) of 1.2 mm wire
4¾ in (12 cm) of 0.5 mm wire
Three black freshwater pearls
Three white freshwater pearls

TECHNIQUES

Purchased chain, page 100
Purchased clasps, page 101
Jump rings, page 104
Music note charm, page 115
Drilling a charm, page 118
Hammering, page 120
Looped top charm, page 121
Attaching charms directly, page 125
Attaching charms and clasps with jump
    rings, page 126

~ Musical Bracelet ~

TO MAKE

Make the 1.5 mm wire into seven jump rings. Attach the clasp and a ring to the ends of the chain. Make the 1.2 mm wire into five musical notes: follow the instructions for the two treble clefs. Follow the photograph for the other three notes, curling the ends of lengths of wire and hammering it. Drill holes in the hammered areas to hang the notes from. Use the 0.5 mm wire and the pearls to make six looped top charms and attach them directly to the chain. Attach the notes with jump rings, spacing all the charms evenly.

Musical ~ Earrings ~

TO MAKE

Make the 0.8 mm wire into two simple ear wires and the 1.2 mm wire into two music notes. Hang the notes from the ear wires. Use the 0.5 mm wire to make the beads and keys into multi-piece charms, following the photograph.

MATERIALS

3½ in (9 cm) of 0.8 mm wire
5½ in (14 cm) of 1.2 mm wire
3 in (8 cm) of 0.5 mm wire
Two small amethyst and two
    small turquoise beads
Two purchased key charms

TECHNIQUES.

Standard ear wires, page 107
Music note charm, page 115
Multi-piece charm, page 123
Looped top and bottom charm,
    page 122
Attaching charms directly, page 125

LEFT: *Dance to the music of time: a musical notes charm bracelet that makes a perfect present for a musician, or for anybody in tune with life.*

RIGHT: *These pretty earrings can just be a gift to a good friend, though the combination of keys and notes would make them powerfully symbolic for someone who has just passed a music exam with flying colors.*

⇜ Simple Silver Necklace ⇝

Materials
2 in (5 cm) 1.5 mm wire
Small trigger clasp
17½ in (44 cm) of medium
    silver curb chain
⅝-in (15-mm) diameter disc
Scrap of open-weave fabric
Purchased heart charm, or
    2 in (5 cm) of 1.5 mm wire
Purchased seahorse charm

Techniques
Purchased chain, page 100
Purchased clasps, page 101
Jump rings, page 104
Wire heart charm, page 113
Disc charm, page 118
Drilling a charm, page 118
Using fabrics, page 119
Attaching charms and clasps
    with jump rings, page 126

To make
Make one length of wire into five jump rings. Attach the clasp and a ring to the ends of the chain. Drill a hole in the disc, then texture it with the fabric. If you are not using a purchased heart charm, make a heart with the other length of wire. Attach the charms to the chain, but slip the rings right over the chain (not through a link) so that they move freely.

RIGHT: *Celebrate a dear friend's silver wedding anniversary with a gift of a stunning solid silver necklace. The charms have been chosen for their symbolic value as well as their good looks: the disc for eternity; the heart, love and feminine energy; and the seahorse, confidence and male energy.*

Cell Phone Charm

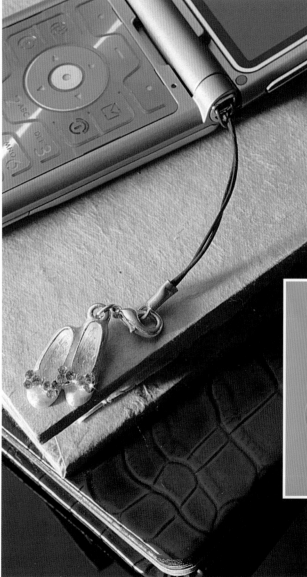

MATERIALS
4¾ in (12 cm) of very thin
    leather cord
Purchased silver end clip
½ in (1 cm) 1.2 mm wire
Purchased shoe charm
Small trigger clasp

TECHNIQUES
Purchased clasps, page 101
Jump rings, page 104
Attaching charms and clasps
    with jump rings, page 126

TO MAKE
Fold the cord in half and slip both ends into the clip. Using flat-nosed pliers, squeeze the top of the clip tightly closed to hold the cord in place. Make the wire into a jump ring and use it to attach the shoe charm to the clasp. Clip the clasp onto the end clip.

LEFT AND ABOVE: *A dainty, yet simple and quick to make, charm for today's "must have" accessory, the cell phone. The dangling fairy-tale shoes will please any style-conscious girl.*

✍ 21st Birthday Girl ✍

MATERIALS

3¼ in (8 cm) of 1.5 mm wire
Small trigger clasp
7 in (18 cm) of medium
    belcher chain
4 in (10 cm) of 0.5 mm wire
Two large green
    freshwater pearls
Two green garnet beads
Three purchased large and
    two small key charms
Two purchased heart charms
    and one star charm

TECHNIQUES

Purchased chain, page 100
Purchased clasps, page 101
Jump rings, page 104
Curly headpin, page 105
Looped top charm, page 121
Attaching charms directly,
    page 125
Attaching charms and clasps
    with jump rings, page 126

TO MAKE

Make the 1.5 mm wire into eight jump rings. Attach the clasp and a ring to the ends of the chain. Attach the star charm to the end ring with another jump ring. Use the 0.5 mm wire and the pearls and stones to make four looped top charms with curly ends and attach them directly to the chain, following the photograph. Put one heart and small key onto each of two rings and attach these and the large keys to the chain, spacing all the charms evenly.

ABOVE: *Strung with symbolic keys to adulthood, freedom, and life, this bracelet makes an ideal gift for a 21st birthday.*

⊱ Evening Bag Charm ⊰

MATERIALS

2¾ in (7 cm) of 1.5 mm wire
Large trigger clasp
8 in (20 cm) of 0.5 mm wire
2 in (5 cm) of medium
    belcher chain
One lapis scarab
Four small lapis stars
Four small lapis hearts
One large lapis heart

TECHNIQUES

Purchased chain, page 100
Purchased clasps, page 101
Jump rings, page 104
Curly headpin, page 105
Looped top charm, page 121
Attaching charms directly,
    page 125
Attaching charms and clasps
    with jump rings, page 126

TO MAKE

Make the 1.5 mm wire into seven jump rings. Attach the clasp to one end of the chain. Make the scarab, two stars, two small hearts, and large heart into six looped top charms; make the remaining stars and hearts into two looped top charms. Attach the scarab to the ring holding the clasp and use the remaining rings to attach the charms to the chain, positioning the large heart and one star at the bottom, following the photograph.

ABOVE: *A sweet little bag charm, ideal for decorating a small evening purse. The charms are made of blue lapis lazuli, with a lapis scarab to bring good fortune.*

Chapter Three
Zodiac

ABOVE: *Each Zodiac sign has a birthstone, and pearls are the stone for Gemini (see page 51.)*

In Western astrology each of the signs of the Zodiac has both a stone and a symbol associated with it, making these signs perfect candidates for charm jewelry that is both beautiful and meaningful. Chinese astrology uses symbolic animals which can also be expressed through jewelry. You will find here ideas for all kinds of jewelry, all of which can be personalized by changing the stones to those suitable for the recipient (see page 16 for a list of birthstones). There is a delicate bracelet for an Aquarian, a striking contemporary necklace for a Sagittarian, a pretty ring for a Gemini, and symbolic earrings for those born under the sign of Pisces.

Amethyst Flower Bracelet

Materials

1½ in (4 cm) of 1.5 mm wire
5½ in (14 cm) of medium
  belcher chain
1½-in (4-cm) diameter carved
  amethyst flower with holes
  on opposite edges
Medium trigger clasp
6 in (15 cm) of
  0.5 mm wire
Six green freshwater pearls
One oval green garnet

Techniques

Purchased chain, page 100
Purchased clasps, page 101
Jump rings, page 104
Looped top charm, page 121
Attaching charms directly,
  page 125
Attaching charms and clasps
  with jump rings, page 126

To make

Make the 1.5 mm wire into four jump rings. Cut the chain in half and attach one end of each length to the flower with a jump ring. Attach a clasp and a ring to the ends of the chain. Use the 0.5 mm wire and the pearls and garnet to make looped top charms and attach them directly to the chain, following the photograph.

BELOW AND RIGHT: *Here is the perfect bracelet for an Aquarian who likes a less traditional look: a carved amethyst flower with silver chain, from which hang charms of green freshwater pearls and a green garnet. A feel of spring for a February girl!*

Contemporary Sagittarian Necklace

MATERIALS
67 in (170 cm) of thin, black
   leather thong
Purchased ¾-in (2-cm)
   diameter silver ring
12 in (30 cm) of 0.5 mm wire
Two large oval
   turquoise beads
Six turquoise round beads
One freshwater pearl
Three sea bamboo flat beads
¾ in (2 cm) 1.5 mm wire
9 in (23 cm) of 1.5 mm wire
   for optional coils and clasp

TECHNIQUES
Jump rings, page 104
Multi-piece charm, page 123
Hook clasp, page 102
Attaching charms and clasps
   with jump rings, page 126

TO MAKE
Cut the leather into two pieces, put them together, fold them together, and loop them through the silver ring, following the photograph. Make three multi-piece charms, following the photograph: make one from a large and small turquoise and the pearl; another from two small turquoises and two sea bamboo beads; and a third from one large and three small turquoises and one sea bamboo bead. Make ¾ in (2 cm) of 1.5 mm wire into three jump rings. Thread two charms onto one ring and one on another and attach them to the purchased ring. The leather can be knotted to fasten the ends, or you can make a clasp in the following way. Make 3 in (7.5 cm) of 1.5 mm wire into a coil, as if you were making jump rings. Bend the topmost ring on the coil up at right angles to the rest of the coil. Push the ends of the leather into the bottom of the coil and, using flat-nosed pliers, squash the coil so that it grips the leather tightly. Repeat on the other end of the leather. Make a hook clasp from 2¾ in (7 cm) of wire and attach it to the top loop of one coil: attach a jump ring to the other coil.

LEFT: *A very modern take on a Sagittarian necklace. The turquoise is of different shades of blue as it was mined in different parts of the world. A few sea bamboo beads make this necklace a very bright option for December.*

ABOVE: *In Chinese astrology, jade brings good luck to all the signs. Here it is combined with turquoise to lift the color scheme. Propitious earrings indeed!*

Jade Heart Earrings

MATERIALS

3¼ in (8 cm) of 0.8 mm wire
1½ in (4 cm) of 1.5 mm wire
12¾ in (32 cm) of very fine belcher chain
6 in (15 cm) of 0.5 mm wire
Two ⅝-in (1.5-cm) long jade hearts
Two small jade stars and two ¼-inch (6-mm) jade beads
Two flat Chinese turquoise beads
Two silver key and two silver glasses charms

TECHNIQUES

Purchased chain, page 100
Jump rings, page 104
Standard ear wires, page 107
Curly headpins, page 105
Looped top charm, page 121
Looped top and bottom charm, page 122
Attaching charms directly, page 125
Attaching charms and clasps with jumps rings, page 126

TO MAKE

Make the 0.8 mm wire into standard ear wires and the 1.5 mm wire into four jump rings. Cut the chain in half and cut each length into three pieces of different lengths. Use 0.5 mm wire and large hearts to make looped top and bottom charms and attach three lengths of chain directly to the bottom loop of each. Use 0.5 mm wire and the small stones to make six looped top charms with curly ends and attach one directly to the end of each length of chain, following the photograph. Attach the charms to the chain with jump rings.

41

Chinese Astrology Bracelet

MATERIALS

8¾ in (22 cm) of 1.5 mm wire
6¾ in (17 cm) of heavy
    belcher chain
14 in (35 cm) of 0.5mm wire
4 in (10 cm) of 0.7 mm wire
Two purchased silver
    animal charms
One purchased silver oval
    charm and one large ring
Four large flat oval
    carnelian beads
One round carnelian bead
Four freshwater pearls
One small citrine bead
Four carved shell animal charms

TO MAKE

Make 3½ in (9 cm) of 1.5 mm wire into a T-bar clasp and the remainder into 13 jump rings. Attach the clasp and purchased ring to the ends of the chain. Use the 0.5 mm wire and stones and pearls to make four carnelian and pearl multi-piece charms, one silver animal and carnelian charm, and one silver oval and citrine charm, following the photograph. Use the 0.7 mm wire to make the carved animals into looped top charms. Using jump rings, attach one silver and one carved animal to the ring and space the other charms along the chain.

TECHNIQUES

Purchased chain, page 100
T-bar clasp, page 103
Jump rings, page 104
Looped top charm, page 121
Multi-piece charm, page 123
Attaching charms and clasps
    with jump rings, page 126

ABOVE AND RIGHT: *Tiny animal charms, some in silver and others hand-carved from cowrie shells, are powerful symbols in Chinese astrology.*

Lapis Lazuli Bracelet

MATERIALS

5½ in (14 cm) of 1.5 mm wire
6¾ in (16 cm) of fine
　belcher chain
½-in (1-cm) diameter
　purchased silver ring
18 in (45 cm) of 0.5 mm wire
Five sodalite hearts
16 lapis lazuli hearts
Five small, dark blue
　freshwater pearls
16 small, white
　freshwater pearls

TECHNIQUES

Purchased chain, page 100
Jump rings, page 104
T-bar clasp, page 103
Looped top charm, page 121
Multi-piece charm, page 123
Attaching charms directly,
　page 125
Attaching charms and clasps
　with jump rings, page 126

TO MAKE

Make 3½ in (9 cm) of 1.5 mm wire into a T-bar clasp and the remainder into five jump rings. Attach the clasp and purchased ring to the ends of the chain. Use the 0.5 mm wire and small hearts and pearls to make fifteen lapis and white pearl multi-piece charms; one lapis and white pearl looped top charm and five sodalite and blue pearl multi-piece charms. Attach a lapis, a sodalite and the looped top charm to the purchased ring with jump rings. Attach the other charms directly to the chain, following the photograph.

Amethyst & Fluorite Earrings

MATERIALS

3¼ in (8 cm) of 0.8 mm wire
Two ½ in (12 mm) disc charms
6¼ in (16 cm) of 0.5 mm wire
Two small amethyst hearts
Two baroque amethyst beads
Two purple freshwater pearls
Two fluorite flowers
¾ in (2 cm) of 1.5 mm wire

TECHNIQUES

Jump rings, page 104
Simple ear wires, page 106
Disc charm, page 118
Drilling a charm, page 118
Using fabrics, page 119
Looped top charm, page 121
Looped top and bottom
    charm, page 122
Attaching charms and clasps
    with jump rings, page 126

RIGHT: *The amethyst February birthstone mixes with purple pearls and pale lilac fluorite to create earrings for a lucky Aquarian.*

LEFT: *This delicate bracelet combines shades of blue with the light given by pearls. It is a good alternative to turquoise for Sagittarians, or expensive sapphires for Virgoans.*

TO MAKE

Make the 0.8 mm wire into simple ear wires. Texture the discs and drill opposite holes on the edge. Make the stones into multi-piece charms, following the photograph. Make the pearls into looped top charms and attach them to the bottom loop of the baroque beads. Make the 1.5 mm wire into two jump rings. Thread the discs onto the ear wires and attach the charms with the jump rings.

⇒ Aquarius Bracelet ⇒

MATERIALS

1¼ in (3 cm) of 1.5 mm wire
7 in (18 cm) of fine
    belcher chain
Medium silver trigger clasp
One purchased silver
    heart charm
39 in (100 cm) of 0.5 mm wire
14 amethyst pieces
3 rose quartz pieces
28 pink, lilac, and gray
    freshwater pearls
2 paua shell pieces

TECHNIQUES

Purchased chain, page 100
Purchased clasps, page 101
Looped top charm, page 121
Attaching charms directly,
    page 125
Attaching charms and clasps
    with jump rings, page 126

TO MAKE

Make the 1.5 mm wire into three jump rings. Attach the clasp and a ring to the ends of the chain. Attach the heart charm to the ring with the remaining jump ring. Use the 0.5 mm wire to make each stone and pearl into a looped top charm and attach them directly to the chain, following the photograph and positioning them to produce subtle waves of color.

LEFT AND RIGHT: *A fabulous chunky bracelet for an Aquarian, combining their amethyst birthstone with rose quartz and pearls for love. No one will ever guess how easy it is to make!*

⇌ Libra Earrings ⇌

MATERIALS
4¼ in (12 cm) of 0.8 mm wire
Four pink opal discs
Two 1 x ¼ in (2.5 cm x 4 mm)
    strips of 0.9 mm sheet silver
1½ in (4 cm) of 1.5 mm wire
4 in (10 cm) of 0.5 mm wire
Two small rose quartz hearts
Two pink freshwater pearls

TECHNIQUES
Jump rings, page 104
Standard ear wires, page 107
Drilling a charm, page 118
Using fabrics, page 119
Looped top charm, page 121
Looped top and bottom
    charm, page 122

TO MAKE
Use 3¼ in (8 cm) of the 0.8 mm wire to make standard ear
wires. Use 1½ in (4 cm) of the 0.8 mm wire and the opal
discs to make two looped top and bottom charms,
following the photograph, and hook them onto the ear
wires. Texture the strips of silver and drill a hole in each
end. Grip each end of a strip with flat-nosed pliers and twist
it a half turn. Use the 0.5 mm wire and hearts and pearls to
make four looped top charms. Make the 1.5 mm wire into
four jump rings, and use them to attach one end of a strip
to a disc charm, and attach one heart and one pearl to the
other end.

RIGHT: *Libra's birthstone is opal, and this is usually
represented with the milky opal. However, this pink opal is
equally valid, and offers a pretty alternative.*

❧ Pearl Charm Rings ❧

To make

Measure the finger you want the ring to fit (freezer bag ties are excellent for this purpose), and choose a short piece of dowel of that diameter. Using chain-nosed pliers, bend the ¼ in (4 mm) wire around it, overlapping the ends to make a ring. Use the 0.5 mm wire and pearls to make seven looped top charms. Make the 1.5 mm wire into a jump ring. Cluster the charms onto the jump ring and attach it to the ring, following the photograph.

The alternative below is made in the same way, but the pearls are attached with a short chain of three jump rings to allow them to swing freely.

MATERIALS
4¾ in (12 cm) of ¼-in (4-mm) wide flat rectangular silver wire
½ in (1 cm) of 1.5 mm wire
20 in (50 cm) of 0.5 mm wire
3 black freshwater pearls
4 white freshwater pearls

TECHNIQUES
Jump rings, page 104
Looped top charm, page 121
Attaching charms and clasps with jump rings, page 126

ABOVE AND RIGHT: *Pretty gifts for a Gemini, these pearl rings are also simple and quick to make. Choose pearls in the recipient's favorite color to make the ring extra special.*

⇒ Gemini Necklace & Earrings ⇒

NECKLACE MATERIALS
7½ in (19 cm) of 1.5 mm wire
17 in (42 cm) of medium
   belcher chain
1¼ x 1¼ in (3 x 3 cm) of
   0.9mm sheet silver
32 in (80 cm) of 0.5 mm wire
40 white freshwater pearls

NECKLACE TECHNIQUES
Purchased chain, page 100
Jump rings, page 104
Hook clasp, page 102
Flower charm, page 117
Hammering, page 120
Looped top charm, page 121
Attaching charms directly,
   page 125
Attaching charms and clasps
   with jump rings, page 126

TO MAKE NECKLACE
Make 4¾ in (12 cm) of 1.5 mm wire into 11 jump rings and
2¾ in (7 cm) into a hook clasp. Attach the clasp and a ring to
the ends of the chain. Cut a flower out of the sheet silver and
hammer it to texture it. Use the 0.5 mm wire and pearls to
make 40 looped top charms. Cluster five pearl charms onto
each of eight jump rings. Attach a cluster to the center of
the chain and space the remaining clusters and the flower
either side, attaching one to every eighth chain link,
following the photograph.

EARRING MATERIALS
3¼ in (8 cm) of 0.8 mm wire
¼ in (2 cm) of 1.5 mm wire
8 in (20 cm) of 0.5 mm wire
Ten white freshwater pearls
8¾ in (22 cm) of very fine
   belcher chain

EARRING TECHNIQUES
Purchased chain, page 100
Jump rings, page 104
Standard ear wires, page 107
Looped top charm, page 121

TO MAKE EARRINGS
Make the 0.8 mm wire into standard ear wires and the 1.5 mm
wire into two jump rings. Use the 0.5 mm wire and pearls to
make ten looped top charms. Cut the chain in half and cut
each length into three pieces of different lengths. Cluster five
pearls and three pieces of chain onto each jump ring and hang
them from the ear wires.

LEFT AND RIGHT: *The lustrous sheen of the pearls associated with
Gemini is perfect for these pretty, feminine pieces of jewelry.*

Scorpio ⊱ Key Ring ⊰

MATERIALS
1¼ in (3 cm) of 1.5 mm wire
1¾ in (4.5 cm) of medium
 belcher chain
Purchased silver key
 ring finding
Purchased silver key and
 porcupine charms
4¾ in (12 cm) of 0.5 mm wire
Three golden
 freshwater pearls
Seven baroque citrine stones

TECHNIQUES
Purchased chain, page 100
Jump rings, page 104
Looped top charm, page 121
Attaching charms directly,
 page 125
Attaching charms and clasps
 with jump rings, page 126

TO MAKE
Make the 1.5 mm wire into three jump rings. Attach one end of the chain to the key ring and the other end to the porcupine charm. Attach the key charm to the chain, following the photograph. Use 0.5 mm wire and two pearls to make two looped top charms and the remaining pearls and stones to make four more looped top charms. Attach the charms directly to the chain.

LEFT: *This pretty key ring combines the birthstone of Scorpio, citrine, with golden freshwater pearls, which give warmth and depth to the color of the citrine.*

⸙ Pisces Earrings ⸙

MATERIALS

3¼ in (8 cm) of 0.8 mm wire
2 in (5 cm) of 0.5 mm wire
Two small baroque
    aquamarine stones
4¾ in (12 cm) of 1.5 mm wire

TO MAKE

Make the 0.8 mm wire into standard ear wires. Use the 0.5 mm wire and stones to make two looped top charms and attach one to each ear wire. Make the 1.5 mm wire into two fish charms and hammer the heads as well as the tails to make them twinkle in the light. Hang the fish from the ear wires.

TECHNIQUES

Standard ear wires page 107
Fish charm, page 112
Looped top charm, page 121

RIGHT: *These simple yet stunning earrings are light, interesting, eye-catching, and—as they combine the aquamarine birthstone and the fish symbol of Pisces— full of meaning.*

Chapter Four
Color

ABOVE: *Stunning effects can be achieved using stones in shades of one color (see page 63).*
LEFT: *A bold accent color can enhance other, more muted, tones (see page 59).*

Working with color is one of the greatest pleasures in making charm jewelry. There is a fabulous range of colored stones and pearls to choose from, and the possible combinations of colors are as limitless as your imagination. Be bold and experiment with mixing colors you wouldn't usually put together—the results may well be a pleasant surprise. If, on the other hand, you have gone a little too crazy, you can simply change elements to tone down your scheme.

In this chapter you will find designs that make use of softly shifting color changes, others that use rich tones of a single color palette, and yet more that combine bold colors—something for everyone.

Ocean Gems Necklace

MATERIALS

5 in (13 cm) of 2 mm wire
2½ in (6 cm) of 1.5 mm wire
18 in (45 cm) of heavy
    belcher chain
39 in (100 cm) of
    0.5 mm wire
Four lilac freshwater pearls
Seven pink freshwater pearls
Five blue freshwater pearls
One small amethyst star
One small amethyst
    baroque bead
One rectangular amethyst bead
One teardrop amethyst bead
One carved amethyst flower
One large rose quartz heart
One rhodonite star
Two square rhodonite beads
One large flat oval
    rhodonite bead
One small rose quartz heart

One large octagonal rose
    quartz bead
One small rose quartz star
One baroque rhodonite bead
One baroque rose quartz bead
One shell flower
One large flat freshwater pearl
One silver cherub charm
One large flat oval
    kyanite bead
Two small square iolite beads
One blue lace agate bead
One large baroque blue lace
    agate bead
One small blue lace
    agate heart
One blue lace agate star
One small baroque blue lace
    agate bead
Five purchased silver charms

TECHNIQUES

Purchased chain, page 100
Hook clasp, page 102
Jump rings, page 104
Looped top charm, page 121
Multi-piece charm, page 123
Wrapped charm, page 124
Attaching charms directly,
    page 125
Attaching charms and clasps
    with jump rings, page 126

TO MAKE

Make 1½ in (4 cm) of the 2 mm wire into a hook clasp and the remainder into a large jump ring. Make the 1.5 mm wire into six jump rings and attach the hook and large ring to the ends of the chain. The success of this necklace depends on the colors flowing together in a pleasing way, so position the stones around the chain and play around until you are happy with the arrangement. Then use the 0.5 mm wire to make the stones and pearls into looped top and multi-piece charms and the flower into a wrapped charm, and attach them all directly to the chain. Attach the purchased charms with jump rings.

RIGHT AND FAR RIGHT: *As the sun sets over the sea, the blue of the sky slowly turns pink, while the water softens into deep purple. This necklace combines these colors with the treasures of the ocean: the smooth glass of sea-washed "mermaid's tears", iridescent pearls, and silver charms of the ocean's inhabitants.*

Rusty Red Brooch

Materials

8 in (20 cm) of 1.5 mm wire
Carnelian butterfly
1¼ in (3 cm) of medium
    belcher chain
2¾ in (7 cm) of 0.5 mm wire
One large bronze
    freshwater pearl
One round carnelian bead
One baroque
    sea bamboo bead

Techniques

Handmade chain, page 98
Purchased chain, page 100
Jump rings, page 104
Brooch pin, page 108
Looped top charm, page 121
Attaching charms directly,
    page 125
Attaching charms and clasps
    with jump rings, page 126

To make

Make 8 in (20 cm) of the 1.5 mm wire into a brooch pin and the remaining 1¼ in (3 cm) into three jump rings. Join the rings together to make a short chain with the butterfly on one end and the brooch pin on the other end, following the photograph. Use the 0.5 mm wire, beads and pearl to make three looped top charms. Slip one end of the chain onto the brooch pin and attach the charms directly to it.

LEFT: *A confident mix of shades within a single color palette can produce a striking piece of jewelry.*

᤟ Flower Necklace ᤟

MATERIALS

16 in (40 cm) of medium
belcher chain
¼ in (2 cm) of 1.5 mm wire
Medium trigger clasp
20 in (50 cm) of 0.5 mm wire
One large and two medium
oval turquoise beads
Two amazonite flower beads
Two fluorite flower beads
Three dark green
freshwater pearls
Four flat sea bamboo beads
Two large and two smaller flat
paua shell beads
Two medium flat
turquoise beads

TECHNIQUES

Purchased chain, page 100
Purchased clasps, page 101
Jump rings, page 104
Looped top charm, page 121
Multi-piece charm, page 123
Attaching charms directly,
page 125
Attaching charms and clasps
with jump rings, page 126

TO MAKE

Make the 1.5 mm wire into two jump rings and attach the
clasp and a ring to the ends of the chain. Use the 0.5 mm
wire to make the fluorite flowers, smaller shells, and two
pearls into looped top charms. Make the remaining stones
and pearl into seven multi-piece charms, following the
photograph. Attach the charms directly to the chain,
positioning them in a symmetrical arrangement on either
side of the large central charm.

RIGHT: *A stunning necklace covering a whole range of
blues and greens, with bright red accents supplied by the
sea bamboo beads.*

Multi-colored Charm Necklace

MATERIALS

20 in (50 cm) of heavy
  belcher chain
5½ in (14 cm) of 1.5 mm wire
1 x ⅝ in (2.5 x 1.5 cm) and ¾ x
  ⅝ in (2 x 1.5 cm) pieces of
  sheet silver
Two ⅝-in (1.5-cm) silver discs
10 in (25 cm) of 0.5 mm wire
One purchased silver
  lizard charm
Nine small baroque
  turquoise beads
Three small baroque
  amazonite beads
Two small black
  freshwater pearls
Two circular and three square
  flat paua shell beads

TECHNIQUES

Purchased chain, page 100
Hook clasp, page 102
Jump rings, page 104
Heart charm, page 116
Star charm, page 117
Disc charm, page 118
Drilling a charm, page 118
Texturing and shaping,
  page 119
Looped top charm, page 121
Multi-piece charm, page 123
Attaching charms directly,
  page 125
Attaching charms and clasps
  with jump rings, page 126

TO MAKE

Make 2¾ in (7 cm) of the 1.5 mm wire into a hook clasp and the remainder into seven jump rings. Attach the clasp and a ring to the ends of the chain. Make the 1 x ⅝ in (2.5 x 1,5 cm) piece of silver into a heart charm and the other piece into a star. Texture, shape and drill all the silver charms. Other than the heart and lizard, assemble the elements into nine multi-piece and looped top charms, following the photograph. Starting at the center of the chain and working out, attach a charm to every fourth link with a jump ring. Attach the heart, lizard and discs with jump rings and the rest directly.

RIGHT AND FAR RIGHT: *Shapes and colors dance happily together in this stunning piece. Turquoise, amazonite, and freshwater pearls enhance the muted iridescence of the shell.*

Seawater Anklet

Left: This anklet has many shades of blue, from light blue to almost green, to the very deepest colors, just like the sea. A couple of silver charms break up the chromatic scale.

MATERIALS
10⅝ in (27 cm) of 1.5 mm wire
9½ in (24 cm) of medium
    belcher chain
⅝-in (1.5-cm) diameter
    purchased ring
1¼ in (4.5 cm) of 1.2 mm wire
16 in (40 cm) of 0.5 mm wire
30 pieces of two colors
    of turquoise
1 green freshwater pearl
10 amazonite beads
One purchased silver charm

TECHNIQUES
Purchased chain, page 100
Hook clasp, page 102
Jump rings, page 104
Curly headpin, page 105
Looped top charm, page 121
Multi-piece charm, page 123
Attaching charms directly,
    page 125
Attaching charms and clasps
    with jump rings, page 126

TO MAKE
Make 2¾ in (7 cm) of the 1.5 mm wire into a hook clasp and the remainder into 19 jump rings. Attach the hook and the purchased ring to the ends of the chain. Make the 1.2 mm wire into a star charm. Use the 0.5 mm wire and stones to make eighteen looped top and multi-piece charms with curly ends, following the photograph. Using jump rings, attach four small stone charms to the large ring and all the rest to the chain, ensuring an even distribution of the different colored stones.

Bead Bookmark

Below: Less can be more: salvaged from an old necklace, this single beautifully colored bead is an effective accent to textured sheet silver.

MATERIALS
5¾ x ⅝ in (14½ cm x 1.5cm)
    piece of 0.9 mm
    sheet silver
12 in (30 cm) of thin, black
    leather cord
Ceramic bead

TECHNIQUES
Sawing sheet silver, page 97
Filing, page 97
Polishing, page 97
Drilling a charm, page 118
Hammering, page 120

TO MAKE
Draw the bookmark shape (see template on page 127) onto the sheet silver and saw it out. Hammer the silver to texture it and file and polish the edges. Drill a hole at one end and loop the leather cord through it. Thread on the bead and tie the ends of the cord in an overhand knot, following the photograph.

Green Key Ring

MATERIALS
2½ in (6.5 cm) of 1.5 mm wire
Purchased silver key
    ring finding
1¼ in (3 cm) of medium
    belcher chain
Carved aventurine flower with
    hole drilled in one petal
4 in (10 cm) of 0.5 mm wire
Aventurine teardrop bead
Two amazonite beads
One serpentine bead
One green freshwater pearl
One silver shoe charm

TECHNIQUES
Purchased chain, page 100
Jump rings, page 104
Looped top charm, page 121
Attaching charms directly,
    page 125
Attaching charms and clasps
    with jump rings, page 126

TO MAKE
Make 1½ in (4 cm) of 1.5 mm wire into a large jump ring and the remaining 1 in (2.5 cm) into two small jump rings. Attach the key ring to one end of the chain with a small ring and the flower to the other end with the large ring. Use the 0.5 mm wire and stones and pearl to make five looped top charms and attach them directly to the chain, following the photograph. Attach the shoe charm using the remaining jump ring.

LEFT: A fresh-looking key ring with a beautiful carved aventurine flower and other beads in shades of soft green.

Autumn Bracelet

RIGHT: Just a few stone charms hang from this simple bracelet, but the careful color choices make it so striking.

MATERIALS
7 in (18 cm) of 1.5 mm wire
5½ in (14 cm) of medium
    belcher chain
⅝-in (1.5-cm) diameter
    purchased ring
5½ in (14 cm) of 0.5 mm wire
Two brown freshwater pearls
One brown stick freshwater
    pearl
One banded agate cylinder
    bead
Two baroque amber beads
One baroque carnelian bead

TECHNIQUES
Purchased chain, page 100
T-bar clasp, page 103
Jump rings, page 104
Looped top charm, page 121
Attaching charms directly,
    page 125
Attaching charms and clasps
    with jump rings, page 126

TO MAKE
Make 3½ in (9 cm) of the 1.5 mm wire into a T-bar clasp and the remainder into nine jump rings. Cut the chain into five equal lengths then join the pieces together with jump rings. Attach a ring to each end of the chain and attach the clasp and purchased ring to these with two more jump rings. Use the 0.5 mm wire and pearls and stones to make five looped top charms, two containing two elements, following the photograph. Attach one charm directly to each of the four central jump rings and the remaining one to the large ring with the final jump ring.

MATERIALS

4 in (10 cm) of 1.5 mm wire
7½ in (19 cm) of medium
   belcher chain
One purchased ⅝-in (1.5-cm)
   diameter ring and two
   silver charms
23 in (58 cm) of 0.5 mm wire
Nine large green pearls
Eleven small green pearls
One small oval green garnet
Six rectangular faceted
   green garnets

TECHNIQUES

Purchased chain, page 100
T-bar clasp, page 103
Jump rings, page 104
Curly headpin, page 105
Looped top charm, page 121
Multi-piece charm, page 123
Attaching charms directly,
   page 125
Attaching charms and clasps
   with jump rings, page 126

Garnet & Green
⇒ Pearl Charm Bracelet ⇐

TO MAKE

Make 1¼ in (4.5 cm) of the 1.5 mm wire into a T-bar clasp and the remainder into five jump rings. Attach the clasp and the purchased ring to the ends of the chain. Use the 0.5 mm wire, three small pearls, small garnet, and one large pearl to make five looped top charms. Cluster them onto one jump ring, and attach them to the purchased ring. Make the remaining pearls into eight multi-piece charms with curly ends and the garnets into six looped top charms with curly ends. Attach these charms directly to the chain and attach the silver charms with jump rings, following the photograph.

RIGHT: *Looking at this bracelet you can feel spring approaching: a mixture of tender green shades from freshwater pearls and green garnet stones. A few silver charms finish off the bracelet.*

Turquoise & Pearl Necklace

MATERIALS
13¼ in (34 cm) of fine
belcher chain
18 in (45 cm) of 0.5 mm wire
Four ¼ in (6 mm) turquoise
round beads
Six ⅛ in (4 mm) turquoise
round beads
Small trigger clasp
Seven gray and ten white
freshwater pearls

TECHNIQUES
Purchased chain, page 100
Purchased clasps, page 101
Looped top charm, page 121
Looped top and bottom
charm, page 122
Attaching charms directly,
page 125

TO MAKE
Cut the chain into two 5½ in (14 cm) and three ¾ in (2 cm) pieces. Use the 0.5 mm wire and two large and four small beads to make two looped top and bottom charms: attach one end directly to a long length of chain and the other end to a short length, so that the charm joins the chains together. Make two small beads into looped top and bottom charms, one with a large loop at one end. Attach a small loop to the ends of the long chains; to the other small loop attach the clasp, so that it closes onto the large loop. Make a large bead into a looped top and bottom charm; attach the top loop to the free short ends of chain (completing the circle), and attach the remaining short length of chain to the bottom loop. Make the final bead into a looped top charm and attach it to the end of the short length. Make all the pearls into looped top charms and attach them directly to the chain, following the photograph.

ABOVE: *The delicate white and gray freshwater pearl charms reflect light and give more depth to the bright blue Mexican turquoise beads.*

Polished Pebble Bag Charm

MATERIALS

4½ in (11 cm) of very heavy
  belcher chain
2¾ in (7 cm) of heavy
  belcher chain
1½ in (4 cm) of 2 mm wire
One very large bolt ring
4 in (10 cm) of 1.5 mm wire
10 in (25 cm) of 0.5 mm wire
One small carnelian heart
Two cylinder agate beads
One teardrop flat jasper bead
Three round flat bronze
  freshwater pearls
One bronze stick
  freshwater pearl
One large flat oval jasper bead
One baroque carnelian bead
One rhodonite star
One purchased silver
  glasses charm
1¼ x ¾ in (3 x 2 cm) of
  0.9 mm sheet silver

TECHNIQUES

Purchased chain, page 100
Jump rings, page 104
Looped top charm, page 121
Multi-piece charm, page 123
Attaching charms and clasps
  with jump rings, page 126

TO MAKE

Make the 2 mm wire into one large jump ring and attach an end of both chains to the bolt ring with it. Make the 1.5 mm wire into ten jump rings. Use the 0.5 mm wire and stones and pearls to make three multi-piece charms and five looped top charms, following the photograph. Make a heart charm from the sheet silver and shape it. Attach all the charms to the chains with jump rings.

LEFT AND RIGHT: *Pebbles, beads, and stars in warm earth tones combine in this bag charm. The silver chains and charms accentuate the rich colors of the stones.*

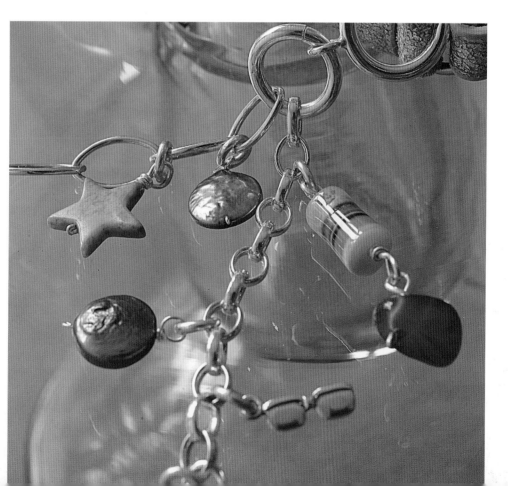

Shell Earrings

MATERIALS
2 in (5 cm) of 0.8 mm wire
Two flat square paua
    shell beads
6¾ in (17 cm) of fine
    belcher chain
Four small Chinese
    turquoise beads
Four dark green
    freshwater pearls
7 in (18 cm) of 0.5 mm wire

TECHNIQUES
Purchased chain, page 100
Curly ear wires, page 107
Looped top charm, page 121
Looped top and bottom
    charm, page 122

TO MAKE
Make the 0.8 mm wire into curly ear wires. Cut the chain into two 2 in (5 cm) and two 1⅜ in (3.5 cm) lengths. Use the 0.5 mm wire and shell beads to make two looped top and bottom charms and attach one of each length of chain to the bottom loops. Hang the top loops from the ear wires. Make the remaining beads and pearls into eight looped top charms and attach them directly to the chains, following the photograph.

RIGHT: *Paua shell is wonderful in terms of color as it contains so many different tones. Here, the cool green and dark shades are picked up by the small beads.*

Silky Lariat Necklace

MATERIALS

56 in (140 cm) silk cord
4¾ in (12 cm) of 1.5 mm wire
11 in (28 cm) of 0.7 mm wire
Six flat oval jasper beads
Four round carnelian beads
One square jasper bead
Two pale gold
   freshwater pearls
One small tourmaline bead

TECHNIQUES

Jump rings, page 104
Curly headpins, page 105
Looped top charm, page 121
Attaching charms and clasps
   with jump rings, page 126

TO MAKE

Tie single knots close to the ends of the cord and ten more knots, randomly spaced, following the photograph. Make the 1.5 mm wire into twelve jump rings, Use the 0.7 mm wire and the beads and pearls to make 14 looped top charms with curly ends. Cluster one pearl, one round carnelian bead and the small tourmaline bead onto a jump ring and attach it to an end knot. Attach the other charms to the knots with jump rings.

RIGHT: *The rich color of the cord and the stone and pearl charms complement each other perfectly in this innovative lariat necklace.*

Plaited Leather Necklace

MATERIALS

78 in (200 cm) of thin, black
  leather cord
15 in (37.5 cm) of
  1.5 mm wire
Large trigger clasp
2⅜ in (6.5 cm) of 1.2 mm wire
15 in (37.5 cm) of
  0.5 mm wire
One large paua shell flower
Three paua shell flat beads
One fluorite flower bead
Two flat turquoise beads
One oval turquoise bead
One small freshwater pearl
Two stick freshwater pearls
Two purchased silver charms

TECHNIQUES

Purchased clasps, page 101
Jump rings, page 104
Fish charm, page 112
Wire heart charm, page 113
Music note charm, page 115
Looped top charm, page 121
Multi-piece charm, page 123
Wrapped charm, page 124
Attaching charms and clasps
  with jump rings, page 126

BELOW AND RIGHT: *A chic take
on an ethnic look: this long
plaited leather necklace
displays a series of shell,
pearl, and stone charms in
shades of blue, green, and
turquoise, brightened with
silver charms.*

TO MAKE

Cut the leather cord into three and make a plait. Use 6 in
(15 cm) of the 1.5 mm wire to make coiled ends (see
Contemporary Sagittarian Necklace, page 40.) Make 4¾ in
(12 cm) of 1.5 mm wire into twelve jump rings and use one
to attach the clasp to one of the coiled ends. With the
remaining 4¼ in (10.5 cm) of wire, make a fish and a heart
charm. Use the 1.2 mm wire to make a music note charm.
Use 6 in (15 cm) of the 0.5 mm wire to wrap the shell
flower, then combine this with a flat shell bead to make a
multi-piece charm, following the photograph. Make the
fluorite flower into a looped top charm and the remaining
pearls, stones, and shell into four multi-piece charms.
Attach all of the charms to the plait with jump rings,
spacing them evenly.

Chapter Five

Protection & Healing

LEFT: *Mix appropriate charms for a traveller with protective stones to make a powerful and witty piece of jewelry (see page 79).*
RIGHT: *An* Oriental *good luck token on a pretty bracelet (see page 83).*
FAR LEFT: *Amazonite in these earrings provides protection against harmful cell phone emissions (see page 80).*

Many charms have a symbolic meaning (see page 11), and many stones have special qualities attributed to them (see page 12), and both of these can be used to give meaning as well as beauty to your pieces of charm jewelry. This chapter looks at the powers of protection and healing you can invest your jewelry with by using specific stones and silver charms.

Use rose quartz to make the prettiest pink necklace that can also bring love and peacefulness to the wearer, or offer protection from the emissions of today's technology with fluorite and amazonite. Choose a silver key charm to help with a new start in life, or a lizard to promote creative dreams.

Butterfly Bag Charm

MATERIALS

1½ in (4 cm) of 2 mm wire
1¼ in (3 cm) of 1.5 mm wire
One very large bolt ring
7 in (18 cm) of heavy
    belcher chain
One large rose quartz butterfly
10 in (25 cm) of 0.5 mm wire
One large baroque rose
    quartz bead
Two baroque rhodonite beads
One oval fluorite bead
One large purple
    freshwater pearl
Two small pink
    freshwater pearls
One baroque amethyst bead
One small blue lace
    agate bead
One purchased teddy bear
    and one butterfly charm

TECHNIQUES

Purchased chain, page 100
Jump rings, page 104
Looped top charm, page 121
Attaching charms directly,
    page 125
Attaching charms and clasps
    with jump rings, page 126

TO MAKE

Make the 2 mm wire into a large jump ring and the 1.5 mm wire into three small jump rings. Cut the chain into two different-length pieces and attach them to the bolt ring with a single jump ring. Attach the stone butterfly to the end of one chain with the large jump ring. Use the 0.5 mm wire and stones and pearls to make five looped top and multi-piece charms, following the photograph. Attach these directly to the chains and attach the silver charms with jump rings.

LEFT AND RIGHT: *Stones to calm the senses and protect against stress make this a perfect bag charm for today's career woman.*

Charm Belt

MATERIALS

3 yds (3 m) of medium black
   leather cord
Large trigger clasp
17 in (43 cm) of
   1.5 mm wire
16 in (40 cm) of 1.2 mm wire
20 in (50 cm) of 0.7 mm wire
Six rose quartz baroque beads
Four pink stick pearls
Three oval rhodonite beads
Ten medium rhodonite
   baroque beads
Three rhodonite cylinders
One round rhodonite bead
One pink tourmaline
   freeform bead
One small round rose
   quartz bead

One rose quartz heart
One small oval rose
   quartz bead
One very small pink
   freshwater pearl
Three purchased silver charms

TECHNIQUES

Jump rings, page 104
Fish charm, page 112
Music note charm, page 115
Looped top charm, page 121
Multi-piece charm, page 123
Attaching charms and clasps
   with jump rings, page 126

TO MAKE

Cut the cord into three and make a plait. Use 6 in (15 cm) of the 1.5 mm wire to make coiled ends (see Contemporary Sagittarian Necklace, page 40.) Make the remainder into 26 jump rings, and use one to attach the clasp to one of the coiled ends. Use the 1.2 mm wire to make five music note charms and one fish charm. Use the 0.7 mm wire and the stones and pearls to make 16 looped top and multi-piece charms: these can use any combination of elements as long as the colors and shapes work well together. Attach all the charms to the belt with jump rings, spacing them along its length.

BELOW: *Surround yourself, quite literally, with protective stones, with this powerful yet very fashionable belt.*

Traveler's Bag Charm

MATERIALS

3¼ in (8 cm) of 1.5 mm wire
Very large trigger clasp
4 in (10 cm) of heavy
    belcher chain
4 in (10 cm) of 0.5 mm wire
One lapis lazuli heart
One sodalite heart
One small round Mexican
    turquoise bead
One large baroque Chinese
    turquoise bead
Four purchased travel-
    theme charms

TECHNIQUES

Purchased chain, page 100
Purchased clasps, page 101
Jump rings, page 104
Looped top charm, page 121
Multi-piece charm, page 123
Attaching charms and clasps
    with jump rings, page 126

TO MAKE

Make the 1.5 mm wire into
eight jump rings and use
one to attach the clasp to
one end of the chain. Use
the 0.5 mm wire and heart
stones to make a multi-piece
charm. Make two looped
top charms from the
remaining stones. Attach
all the charms to the chain
with jump rings, following
the photograph.

RIGHT AND ABOVE: *A bag charm for setting out on a journey. The lapis lazuli and turquoise are there to protect and calm the traveler, as well as to encourage them to take charge of life.*

Pretty Pink Necklace

MATERIALS

4½ in (11 cm) of 1.5 mm wire
16 in (40 cm) of fine
    belcher chain
6 in (15 cm) of 0.5 mm wire
One small rose quartz heart
    and one bead
One large octagonal rose
    quartz bead
Two pink freshwater pearls
One purchased silver leaf and
    one star charm

TECHNIQUES

Purchased chain, page 100
Hook clasp, page 102
Jump rings, page 104
Looped top charm, page 121
Multi-piece charm, page 123
Attaching charms directly,
    page 125
Attaching charms and clasps
    with jump rings, page 126

TO MAKE

Make 2¾ in (7 cm) of the 1.5 mm wire into a hook clasp and the remainder into four jump rings. Attach the hook and a jump ring to the ends of the chain. Use the 0.5 mm wire and the stones and pearls to make two multi-piece charms; one with the large rose quartz bead and heart and a pearl, and the other with a pearl and bead. Attach the large charm directly to the center of the chain and space the other charms either side, attaching the silver ones with jump rings.

Amazonite Earrings

LEFT: If you spend time on your cell phone, amazonite, to absorb phone emissions, is a good choice for earrings.

RIGHT: Rose quartz helps to calm frayed nerves and bring peace to the senses, so wear it during times of stress. A scattering of other charms makes it a beautiful as well as practical piece.

MATERIALS

3½ in (9 cm) of 0.8 mm wire
4 in (10 cm) of 0.7 mm wire
Six amazonite discs
4 in (10 cm) of 0.5 mm wire
Two ¼ in (6 mm) and two ⅛ in
    (4 mm) amazonite
    round beads
Two flat turquoise beads
Two small blue
    freshwater pearls
Two blue pearl discs
3¼ in (8 cm) of fine
    belcher chain

TECHNIQUES

Purchased chain, page 100
Standard ear wires, page 107
Looped top charm, page 121
Attaching charms directly,
    page 125

TO MAKE

Make the 0.8 mm wire into standard ear wires. Cut the chain in half. Use the 0.7 mm wire and amazonite discs to make two looped top charms, each with three discs, and a length of chain hanging from the bottom. Hang the charms from the ear wires. Use the 0.5 mm wire and remaining stones and pearls to make ten looped top charms. Attach them directly to the chain, following the photograph.

~ Oriental-style Bracelet ~

MATERIALS
8 in (20 cm) of 1.5 mm wire
One ⅝-in (1.5-cm) diameter
    purchased ring
6¼ in (17 cm) of heavy
    belcher chain
16 in (40 cm) of 0.5 mm wire
Three round turquoise beads
Three small lapis lazuli stars
    and one heart
One very large
    multi-colored bead
One small red crystal bead
Two large silver beads
Three large blue beads
One flat silver *pa kua* charm
Two filigree charms

TECHNIQUES
Purchased chain, page 100
T-bar clasp, page 103
Jump rings, page 104
Multi-piece charm, page 123
Attaching charms and clasps
    with jump rings, page 126

TO MAKE
Make 3½ in (9 cm) of the 1.5 mm wire into a t-bar clasp and the remainder into 11 jump rings. Attach the clasp and large ring to the ends of the chain. Make the beads into multi-piece charms, following the photograph. Attach all the charms to the chain with jump rings, spacing them evenly.

LEFT AND RIGHT: *This bracelet is composed of beads and silver pieces salvaged from old jewelry. Choose items that will have meaning for the wearer, such as a bead from a favorite, but now broken, necklace, and top them off with a* pa kua *charm, an oriental symbol of good luck.*

⇒ Dream Necklace ⇒

MATERIALS

20 in (50 cm) of medium
    leather cord
4½ in (11 cm) of 1.5 mm wire
1⅜-in (3.5-cm) diameter disc
2½ in (6 cm) of
    0.5 mm wire
One blue lace agate star
One small pink
    freshwater pearl
One purchased lizard and
    one porcupine charm

TECHNIQUES

Jump rings, page 104
Drilling a charm, page 118
Using fabrics, page 119
Doming, page 120
Multi-piece charm, page 123
Attaching charms and clasps
    with jump rings, page 126

TO MAKE

Fold one end of the leather over to make a loop and bind it in place with 1¼ in (3 cm) of 1.5 mm wire. (To fasten the necklace, knot the free end through the loop.) Make the remaining 3¼ in (8 cm) of wire into four large jump rings. Texture the disc with fabric and then curve it in a doming block. Drill four holes at the points of the compass, close to the edge, following the photograph. Use the 0.5 mm wire and the stone and pearl to make a multi-piece charm. Attach the charms to the disc and the disc to the cord with jump rings.

ABOVE: *In Native American mythology the porcupine symbolizes innocence and the lizard, dreaming. These properties, combined with the calm of the agate, make this a good necklace for a spiritual, creative person.*

Leaf Charm Bracelet

MATERIALS

6 in (15 cm) of 1.5 mm wire
6 in (15 cm) of medium
   belcher chain
2⅞ x ¾ in (7.5 x 2 cm) piece of
   0.9 mm sheet silver
4¾ in (12 cm) of 0.5 mm wire
Four carved aventurine leaves

TO MAKE

Make 3½ in (9 cm) of the 1.5 mm wire into a T-bar clasp and the remainder into six jump rings. Attach the clasp and purchased ring to the ends of the chain. Draw four leaf shapes, each about ⅝ x 1 in (1½ x 2½ cm) onto the sheet silver. Saw them out, texture them, and drill a hole in the top of each one. Use the 0.5 mm wire and stone leaves to make four looped top charms and attach them directly to the chain, following the photograph. Attach one silver leaf to the large ring and the others to the chain with jump rings.

TECHNIQUES.

Purchased chain, page 100
T-bar clasp, page 103
Jump rings, page 104
Looped top charm, page 121
Attaching charms directly,
   page 125
Attaching charms and clasps
   with jump rings, page 126

LEFT: *Aventurine aids
creativity so,combined with
the leaf symbol of renewal,
this is a great bracelet to give
to an artistic friend.*

85

Flower Necklace

MATERIALS

¼ in (2 cm) of 1.5 mm wire
Small trigger clasp
18½ in (47 cm) of fine
    belcher chain
16½ in (41 cm) of 0.5 mm wire
Seven fluorite flowers
One large amazonite flower
One flat paua shell bead
Three small turquoise beads
Six large dark
    freshwater pearls

TECHNIQUES

Purchased chain, page 100
Purchased clasps, page 101
Jump rings, page 104
Looped top charm, page 121
Multi-piece charm, page 123
Attaching charms directly,
    page 125
Attaching charms and clasps
    with jump rings, page 126

TO MAKE

Make the 1.5 mm wire into two jump rings and attach the clasp and a ring to the ends of the chain. Make the amazonite flower, shell, turquoises, and a fluorite flower into a multi-piece charm, following the photograph, and attach it directly to the center of the chain. Make the remaining fluorite flowers and the pearls into looped top charms and attach them directly to the chain, spacing them out on either side of the central charm.

LEFT AND RIGHT: *The enticing colors make the fluorite flowers look almost edible. This is a great necklace for protection, especially against computer and other electromagnetic stresses.*

Rose Quartz Key Ring

MATERIALS

1¼ in (3 cm) of 1.5 mm wire
Silver key ring finding
2 in (5 cm) fine
    belcher chain
7 in (18 cm) of 0.5 mm wire
One medium pink pearl
One large baroque rose
    quartz bead
One small rose quartz heart
One rose quartz star
Two small rose quartz beads
Two rhodonite beads
One purchased
    butterfly charm

TECHNIQUES

Purchased chain, page 100
Jump rings, page 104
Looped top charm, page 121
Attaching charms directly,
    page 125
Attaching charms and clasps
    with jump rings, page 126

TO MAKE

Make the 1.5 mm wire into three jump rings and attach the chain to the key ring with one of them. Use the 0.5 mm wire and the stones to make eight looped top charms. Using jump rings, attach the large stone to the end of the chain and then attach the butterfly. Attach the rest of the charms directly, following the photograph.

LEFT *An ideal little gift for a dear friend: not only a useful piece, but one that conveys the peace, calm, and love offered by the rose quartz.*

Green Brooch

MATERIALS

9½ in (24 cm) of 1.5 mm wire
3½ in (9 cm) of fine
    belcher chain
12 in (30 cm) of 0.5 mm wire
One large carved
    aventurine flower
One small green
    freshwater pearl
One round amazonite bead
One jade heart
One aventurine teardrop bead
One fluorite bead
Two baroque
    crysoprase beads

TECHNIQUES

Purchased chain, page 100
Jump rings, page 104
Brooch pin, page 108
Looped top charm, page 121
Attaching charms directly,
    page 125
Attaching charms and clasps
    with jump rings, page 126

RIGHT: *Green is good for you! This combination of green stones will absorb negative energies, calm the emotions and help to balance the* yin *and* yang.

TO MAKE

Make 8 in (20 cm) of the 1.5 mm wire into a brooch pin and the remainder into two small and one large jump ring. Cut the chain into two different-length pieces, cluster one end of each onto a small ring and attach them to the pin. Make the small stones and pearl into looped top charms. Cluster the pearl charm, one stone and the flower onto the large ring and attach it to the brooch. Attach one stone to the end of a chain with a large jump ring and attach all the others directly, following the photograph.

Cluster Charm Necklace

MATERIALS
6 in (15 cm) of 1.5 mm wire
3 yds (3 m) of thin, black
   leather cord
8 in (20 cm) of 0.7 mm wire
One malachite cylinder
One baroque turquoise bead
One large baroque
   amazonite bead
One teardrop aventurine bead
One baroque crysoprase bead
One round amazonite bead
One flat round
   freshwater pearl

TECHNIQUES
Jump rings, page 104
Curly headpin, page 105
Multi-piece charm, page 123
Attaching charms and clasps
   with jump rings, page 126

RIGHT: *A stunning selection of green semi-precious stones make this deceptively simple necklace very interesting. Malachite, turquoise, amazonite, aventurine, crysoprase, and freshwater pearls are combined to create a very powerful protective and calming charm.*

TO MAKE
Make 2¾ in (7 cm) of the 1.5 mm wire into a hook clasp, 1¼ in (3 cm) into three small jump rings, and 2 in (5 cm) into one large ring. Cut the leather cord into three pieces, fold them in half, and loop them through the large jump ring. Make coiled ends for the leather (see Contemporary Sagittarian Necklace, page 40.) Slip one side of the hook through one coiled end. Make the stones and pearl into three multi-piece charms with curly ends, following the photograph. Attach the charms to the large ring with jump rings.

Treble-ring Earrings

MATERIALS
3½ in (9 cm) of 0.8 mm wire
8 in (20 cm) of 1.5 mm wire
4¼ in (12 cm) of 0.5 mm wire
Two round aventurine beads
Two square aventurine beads
Two round amazonite beads

TECHNIQUES.
Jump rings, page 104
Standard ear wires, page 107
Looped top charm, page 121
Attaching charms directly,
   page 125

TO MAKE
Make the 0.8 mm wire into standard ear wires. Make the 1.5 mm wire into six large rings (in the same way as you would make jump rings), and fasten them together into two lots of three, following the photograph. Make the stones into six looped top charms and attach them directly to the lower ring. Hang the top ring from the ear wires.

LEFT: *A very modern pair of earrings with amazonite to filter harmful emissions and aventurine to soothe the soul.*

Chapter Six
Techniques

ABOVE: *Learn to make beautiful charms from silver and semi-precious stones, and complement them with handmade findings.*

Making your own jewelry is simpler than you might think, but beware, it is completely addictive! If you are a jewelry novice, you may find some of the techniques take a little practice before you are confident with them, but it really is just a little time time that is needed. Silver wire is not expensive, so cut a few lengths and try making various charms until you get the hang of using the tools to bend the wire smoothly. Take your time, there's no rush, and you will soon be making pieces to be proud of. When making semi-precious stone charms, don't worry if they don't work out well initially: just cut the wire and the stones can be used again.

Tools

You do not need a wide selection of tools to begin making your own charm jewelry and those you do need are not expensive. The collection shown here comprises everything needed to make every single project in this book. Start out by buying the pliers and wire cutters, a fretsaw with spare blades, a flat file, and a polishing block; these are the basic tools you need, the Suppliers list (see page 128) gives stockists of these items. Buy more tools as required as you master more of the techniques.

Wire cutters with sturdy blades for cutting thin and thick silver wire.

Chain-nosed pliers with narrow, pointed tips will help you handle tiny, intricate charms.

Two pairs of flat-nosed pliers with jaws of different widths. Sometimes you will need to hold a piece of wire in two places to manoeuvre it into position, so you will need two pairs of these pliers. The different widths will allow you to hold both tiny and larger pieces of wire securely while working on them.

Two pairs of round-nosed pliers with jaws of different diameters. The different diameters allow you to make rings and curls of different dimensions.

A fretsaw ideal for cutting sheet silver. Buy some spare blades as well, as they do break from time to time.

A scriber is used for drawing shapes (such as hearts and stars) onto sheet silver before cutting them out.

A hand drill is the best tool for drilling holes in sheet silver. A 1.6 mm metal drill bit is a good all-purpose bit to buy. A center punch is used to make a mark that will stop the drill sliding across the silver when drilling a hole.

A flat file, a triangular file, and a round file. The flat file is used for filing edges, the triangular file is useful for notching sheet silver and wire before sawing it, and the round file is for curves and the inside of drilled holes.

A ruler is useful for measuring specific lengths of wire when making charms.

A selection of hammers with different-shaped heads. Left to right: a ball-peen hammer; a corking hammer; a flat-headed hammer. These all produce different textures when used to hammer sheet silver or wire. A steel block is used for hammering onto. This solid surface will give the best results.

A doming block is a metal cube with semi-circular holes of different diameters in the sides. It is used to curve silver shapes. A wooden doming punch and wooden mallet are used with it.

A polishing block is specially formulated to smooth the edges of silver sheet and wire, removing any filing marks, and giving a professional finish.

A jeweller's peg is a useful piece of equipment that clamps onto your work surface. The shaped front edge makes it easier to position and hold small charms while working on them.

☙ Materials ☙

At the front of this book you will find lots of information on the different stones, pearls, and commercially available silver charms used in projects in this book. Other than these, the only materials you need are silver wire, and sheet silver.

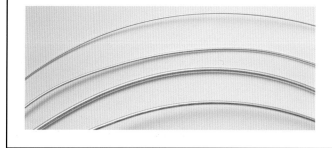

Silver wire is available in a range of gauges (or thicknesses), and those shown are the gauges used in this book.
Top to bottom: 0.5 mm is used for making threaded charms; 0.8 mm is used for making threaded charms of stones with large drilled holes, and for making ear wires; 1.2 mm is the best gauge for making most wire charms; 1.5 mm is used to make some wire charms, handmade chain, jump rings, and all clasps.

Buy 0.9 mm-thick sheet silver for making sheet silver charms. It is easy to saw and polish and responds well to texturing.

Basic Techniques

These are the fundamental techniques that you will use time
and time again in making charm jewelry.

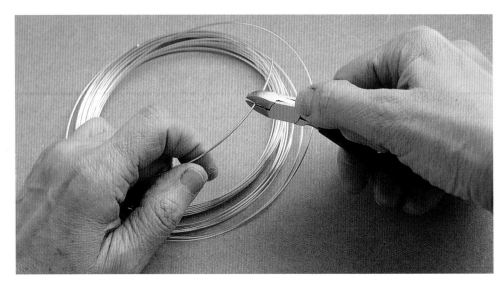

Cutting wire

Use wire cutters to cut pieces
of wire to the required
lengths. Hold the wire
cutters at right angles to the
wire to ensure a clean,
square-cut end.

Filing ends of wire

It is important always to file the ends of wire square
and smooth to remove any sharp points that could
scratch the skin. Hold the wire close to the end to
prevent it from bending while you file. Place a flat file
across the cut end, at right angles to the wire, and rub
back and forth several times. Check that the end does
not feel sharp before proceeding. The only wire that
does not need filing is 0.5 mm wire, as it is so thin.

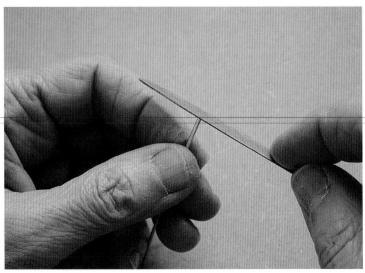

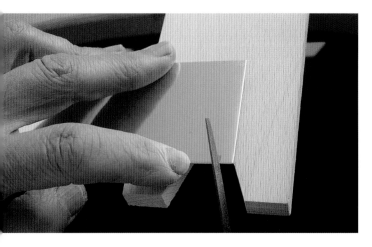

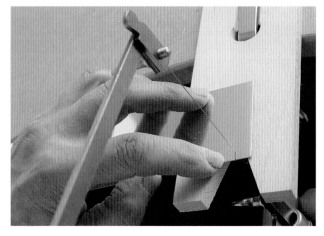

Sawing sheet silver

1 Use a corner of a triangular file to make a small notch in the edge of the sheet silver where you want to start sawing.

2 Keeping the saw at right angles to the metal, start sawing from the notch. The saw cuts on both the upward and downward strokes.

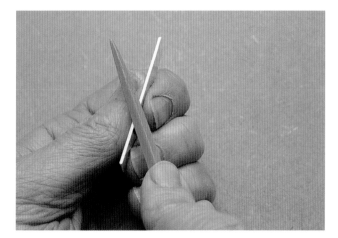

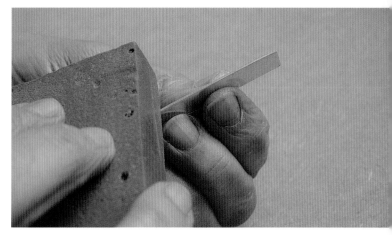

Filing

The sawn edges of sheet silver can be sharp and so must always be filed smooth to prevent them from scratching the skin. Hold a flat file square across the edge of the metal and rub it backwards and forwards across the edge, keeping the pressure even. Check that the edge feels smooth before proceeding.

Polishing

After you have filed the edges of a sheet silver charm, polish them to remove any filing marks. Hold the polishing block square across the edge of the metal and rub the charm back and forth a few times until the marks have disappeared.

Foundation Pieces

These are the basic elements that will, as the name suggests, be the foundation of all of your charm jewelry.

❧ *Handmade Chain* ❧

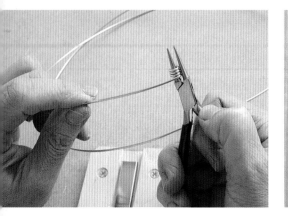

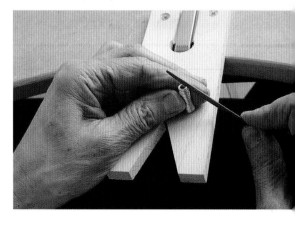

1 Cut a long length of 1.5 mm wire, but do not files the ends. Grip one end of the wire with the base of the jaws of round-nosed pliers. Holding the wire still with your free hand, turn the pliers to coil the wire around one of the jaws. When the wire has bent right around the jaw, turn the pliers inside the coil, ensuring that the free end of the wire is below the coil. Continue coiling in this way, keeping the free end of the wire at the base of the jaws so that it is always bending around the same part of the jaw. This will ensure that all the coils are the same size.

2 Make as many coils as you need links for your chain.

3 Take the coiled wire off the pliers. Holding it still, use a triangular file to make a notch right down one side of the coil.

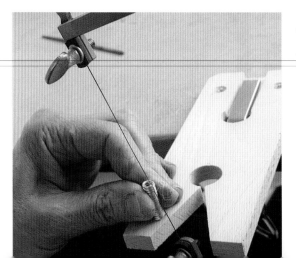

4 Holding the coil upright, saw right through all the links, using the notch as the starting point.

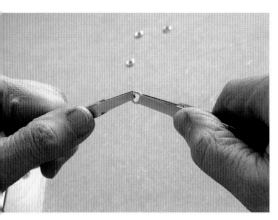

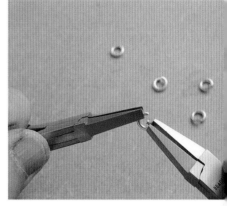

5 Hold both sides of a ring in a pair of flat-nosed pliers. Twist the open ends of the ring past one another in the opposite direction to the way they are lying, then twist them back again so that they are touching one another.

6 Rub your finger over the join to ensure that the ends are flush. If they are not, gently squeeze the join with the pliers to make the ends align with one another perfectly.

7 Hold both sides of a second ring with flat-nosed pliers. Twist the open ends of the ring past one another in the opposite direction to the way they are lying, but do not twist them back to join them.

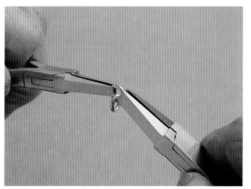

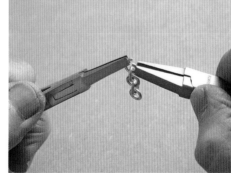

8 Slip the first ring onto the second one. Twist the ends of the second ring so that they are touching. Repeat Step 6 to ensure that the join is perfectly flush.

9 Repeat Steps 7–8 until the chain is the desired length.

ABOVE: *Making your own chain takes a little more time than using purchased chain, but it does lend a lovely quality to a special necklace or bracelet.*

⟨ Purchased Chain ⟩

LEFT: *Though various styles of silver chain are commercially available, those shown here work best for most charm jewelry. Each project tells you the size of chain needed to make it. Top to bottom: very fine belcher chain; fine belcher chain; medium belcher chain; heavy belcher chain.*

LEFT: *Choose a fine chain for a delicate necklace sprinkled with pearls and flower charms.*

RIGHT: *A chunkier chain works well for a bag charm, or a bracelet.*

~ Purchased Clasps ~

LEFT: *There is a wide selection of commercially available clasps that offer secure, and sometimes decorative, fastenings for jewelry. Clockwise from top: heart-shaped trigger clasp; trigger clasp; ring trigger clasp; barrel clasp; large trigger clasp.*

ABOVE: *A decorative clasp, like the heart-shaped one shown here, adds a pretty detail to any piece of jewelry. The other end of the chain has a ring (see Jump Rings, page 104), through which the clasp is closed.*

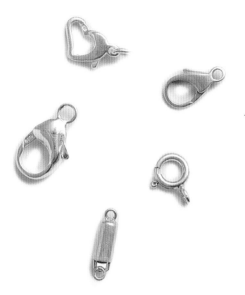

LEFT: *A bag charm needs to be firmly fastened to the bag, so use a large, strong clasp to attach it.*

RIGHT: *Use a clasp, rather than a jump ring, to attach a charm to a cell phone strap, or even a key ring, then you can easily change it as the fancy takes you.*

⇒ Hook Clasp ⇐

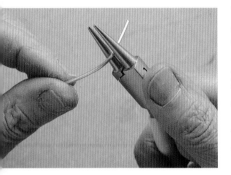

1 For an average-sized clasp, cut 2 ³⁄₄ in (7 cm) of 1.5 mm wire. File the ends smooth (see Filing Ends of Wire, page 96.) Grip one end of the wire with the base of the jaws of round-nosed pliers, ³⁄₄ in (2 cm) from one end. Bend the wire over one of the jaws and back on itself.

ABOVE: Both simple to make and pretty, this clasp also provides a secure fastening for your jewelry. An oversized hook clasp can be a decorative feature in its own right.

2 Bend the other end of the wire in the same way, but in the opposite direction to the first bend, to form the hook's "S" shape.

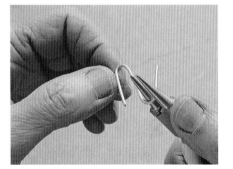

3 One at a time, hold the very ends of the wire in flat-nosed pliers, and gently bend them out a little.

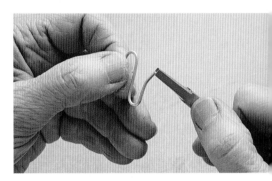

4 Lay the hook on the steel block. Using the ball-pen hammer, hammer both ends of the wire flat.

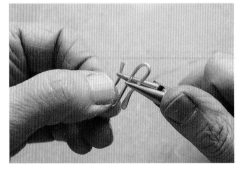

5 Using round-nosed pliers, gently squeeze one side of the hook towards the central section, so that the jump ring attaching the clasp to chain will not slip through the gap.

T-bar Clasp

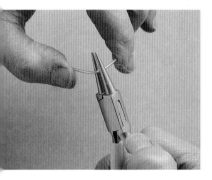

1 For an average-sized clasp, cut 1 ³⁄₄ in (4.5 cm) of 1.5 mm wire. File the ends smooth (see Filing Ends of Wire, page 96.) Grip the middle of the wire close to the tips of round-nosed pliers and bend both ends around one of the jaws, bending them towards one another.

2 Continue bending the ends so they cross over one another.

ABOVE: *This is a striking and contemporary style of clasp. Attach it to a chain with a jump ring through the loop before attaching a purchased ring (large enough for one arm of the clasp at a time to pass through) to the other end of the chain. Here, the ring has been decorated with threaded pearl charms (see Looped Top Charm, page 121) to add interest to the clasp.*

3 Press the ends out until they form a straight line behind the loop of wire around the jaw.

4 Lay the clasp on the steel block. Using the ball-peen hammer, hammer both ends of the wire flat.

~ *Jump Rings* ~

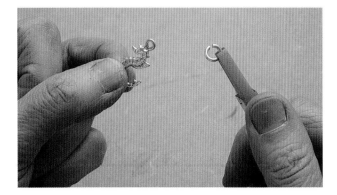

1 Follow Steps 1–4 of Handmade Chain (see page 98), making as many wire coils as you need jump rings. Hold one side of a ring with flat-nosed pliers and pass one end through the hole or loop of a charm.

ABOVE: *Jump rings are the quickest and easiest way to fasten any style of charm to a chain. If you are using a trigger clasp or small hook clasp to fasten the chain, providing the ring that a trigger clasp or small hook clasp fastens to.*

LEFT: *You can cluster several looped top charms (see page 121) onto one jump ring, then attach the ring to a link in a chain, or, as here, to standard ear wires (see page 107.)*

2 Hold both sides of the ring with flat-nosed pliers. Twist the open ends of the ring past one another in the opposite direction to the way they are lying, then twist them back again so that they are touching. Rub your finger over the join to ensure that the ends are flush. If they are not, gently squeeze the join with the pliers to make the ends align perfectly.

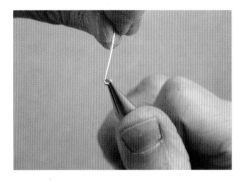

Simple Headpin

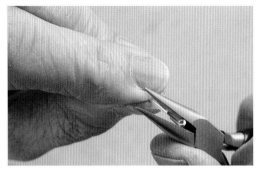

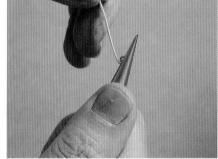

1 The size of a headpin depends entirely on the size of the bead you want to thread on to it. The gauge of wire will also depend on the size of the hole in the bead. However, 1 ³⁄₄ in (4.5 cm) of 0.5 mm wire (for a small hole) or 0.8 mm wire (for a large hole) will make a useful-sized headpin. Grip one end of the wire with the tips of the jaws of chain-nosed pliers and bend it over to make a tiny loop.

2 Squeeze the loop flat with the pliers: this thicker end will prevent the bead sliding off.

ABOVE: *All of these pearls are threaded with this most basic style of headpin to make them into threaded charms (see page 121.)*

Curly Headpin

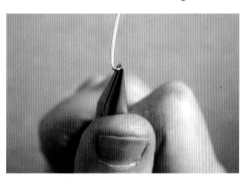

ABOVE: *The little curl adds a delicately stylish touch to threaded charms (see page 121.)*

1 Cut a length of wire as for a simple headpin (see above), and make a loop at one end in the same way.

2 Hold the loop flat in the jaws of the pliers and bend the wire round to make a curl. Move the pliers around and continue bending until the curl is the required size.

Simple Ear Wires

1 Cut 1 ½ in (4 cm) of 0.8 mm wire. File the ends smooth (see Filing Ends of Wire, page 96.) Grip one end of the wire with the tips of the jaws of round-nosed pliers and bend the wire around one of the jaws to make a small loop.

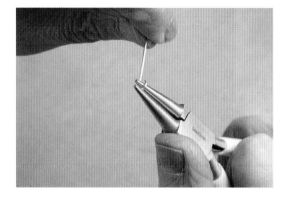

ABOVE: *This is the most basic style of ear wire you can make. Hang charms from the small loop at the front.*

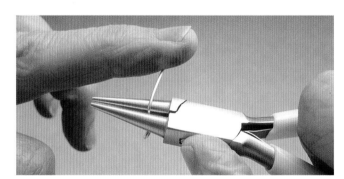

2 Hold the wire in the base of the jaws, just above the loop, and bend it over one of the jaws.

3 Bend the end of the wire right down until it is lying parallel with the looped side.

4 Grip the straight end of the wire with flat-nosed pliers, holding it just above the end. Bend the wire out at a shallow angle.

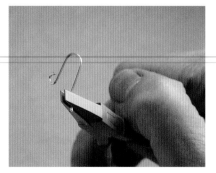

Standard Ear Wires

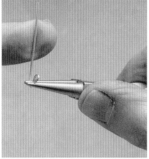

1 Cut 1 ¾ in (4.5 cm) of 0.8 mm wire. File the ends smooth (see Filing Ends of Wire, page 96.) Grip one end of the wire with the tips of the jaws of round-nosed pliers and bend the wire around one of the jaws to make a small loop.

2 Hold the wire in the tips of the jaws, just below the loop. Bend the wire under and around the jaw at the back, so that it stands straight up behind the loop.

3 Follow Steps 2–4 of Simple Ear Wires (see opposite) to complete the ear wire.

ABOVE: *This style of ear wire is probably the most commonly used. Hang charms from the bottom of the lower loop.*

Curly Ear Wires

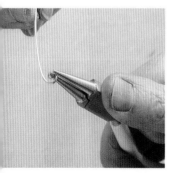

1 Cut 2 in (5 cm) of 0.8 mm wire. File the ends smooth (see Filing Ends of Wire, page 96.) Grip one end of the wire with the tips of the jaws of round-nosed pliers and coil it around one of the jaws. Move the pliers along the wire and continue bending to make a curl (see Curl Charm, page 110.)

2 Follow Steps 2–4 of Simple Ear Wires (see page 106) to complete the ear wire.

ABOVE: *The little curl adds style to the simplest earring design and provides a place to hang a charm from.*

Brooch Pin

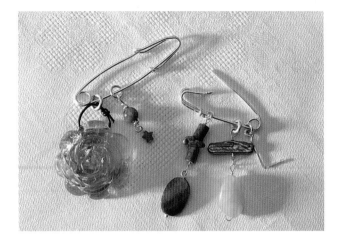

ABOVE: *Hang a myriad of charms from these pins to make an endless variety of brooches.*

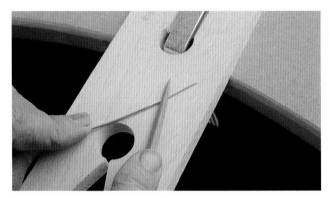

1 Cut approximately 7 in (18 cm) of 1.5 mm wire. Using the flat file, file one end to a sharp point: hold the wire flat on the work surface, and push the file away from you to shape the metal. Turn the wire frequently to create an even, gently tapering point. Test the point to make sure it goes through fabric without damaging it. File the other end of the wire smooth (see Filing Ends of Wire, page 96.)

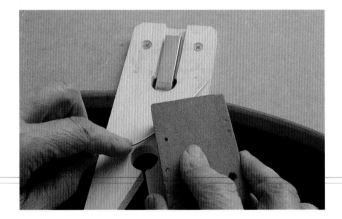

2 Use a polishing block to remove the filing marks from the point (see Polishing, page 97.)

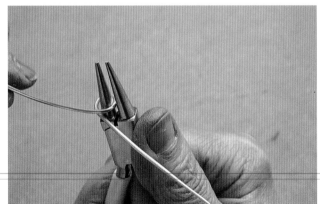

3 Grip the wire in the base of the jaws of round-nosed pliers, about 2 in (5 cm) from the point. Bend both ends around one of the jaws until they cross, then press them out until they form a straight line in front of the loop of wire around the jaw.

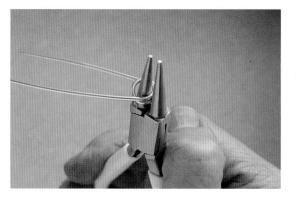

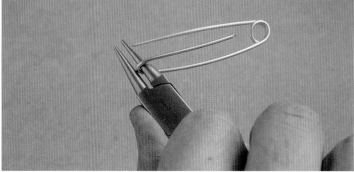

4 Press the ends of the wire around further until they are lying parallel on either side of the loop.

5 Grip the long end of the wire with the base of the jaws, about 2 ½ in (6 cm) above the loop, and bend it back on itself.

6 Hold the wire in chain-nosed pliers ¾ in (2 cm) below the last bend. Bend the wire at right angles, away from the pointed end.

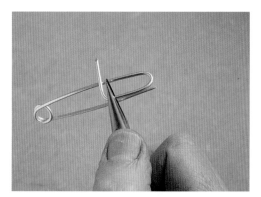

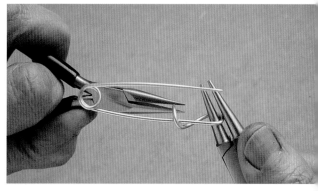

7 Hold the wire in the bend made in Step 5 about halfway up the jaws of round-nosed pliers. Grip the end beyond the right-angled bend with chain-nosed pliers and pull the right-angled bend tight against the wire it is facing. Wrap the end around this section of wire.

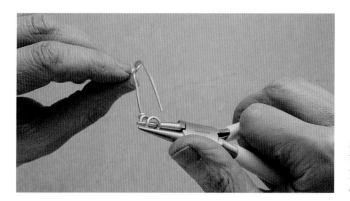

8 Using round-nosed pliers, bend the end of the wrapped loop over to form the clasp end of the brooch pin.

Wire Charms

Silver wire can be used to create pretty, delicate handmade charms to dangle from your jewelry. All these pieces are simple to make and yet look so effective.

RIGHT: *Use these curls as charms in their own right (right), or join them to other elements to make more complex charms (see Multipiece Charm, page 123.)*

Curl Charm

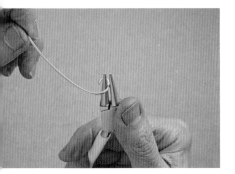

1 Cut 3 ¼ in (8 cm) of 1.5 mm wire. File the ends smooth (see Filing Ends of Wire, page 96.) Grip one end of the wire close to the tips of round-nosed pliers. Hold the other end of the wire with your free hand and turn the pliers to curl the wire.

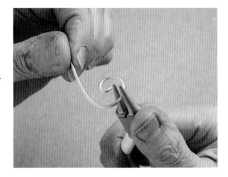

2 Move the pliers along the wire and continue bending it to create the curl.

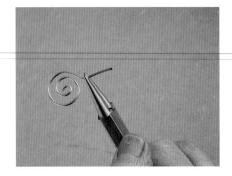

3 When you are ½ in (1 cm) from the end of the wire, use chain-nose pliers to bend the wire at a right angle away from the curl.

4 Using the tips of round-nosed pliers, bend the end of the wire to form a small loop.

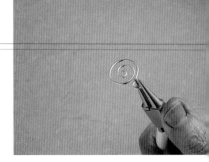

S-curl Charm

RIGHT: *Wire charms can be given an extra dimension by hammering them to create surface texture (see Hammering, page 120.) Just slip a jump ring through one end of this spiralling charm to attach it to a chain.*

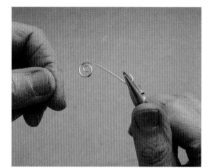

1 Cut 3 ½ in (8 cm) of 1.2 mm wire. File the ends smooth (see Filing Ends of Wire, page 96.) Follow Steps 2–3 of Curl Charm (see opposite) to make a curl in one end.

2 When you have curled about half the wire, curl the other end in the same way, but in the opposite direction. Ensure that at the middle of the "S" the curls are tight enough to stop a jump ring passing through.

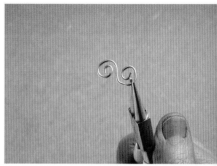

Square S-curl Charm

ABOVE: *The geometric shape of this charm complements to a contemporary piece of jewelry well.*

1 Cut 4¾ in (12 cm) of 1.2 mm wire. File the ends smooth (see Filing Ends of Wire, page 96.) Using chain-nosed pliers, bend the wire in a series of right angles to form three sides of a small square.

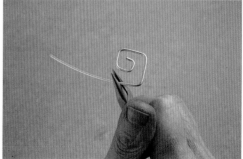

2 Make the next bend further away from the first side of the small square, so that you start to form a square coil. Continue bending in this way. When you have bent about half the wire, bend the other end in the same way, but in the opposite direction.

Hammered Spike Charm

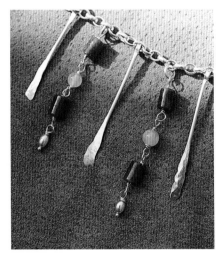

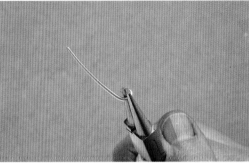

1 Cut 1½ in (4 cm) of 1.5 mm wire. File the ends smooth (see Filing Ends of Wire, page 96.) Grip one end of the wire with the tips of round-nosed pliers and bend it around one of the jaws to form a loop.

Above: *The simplicity of hammered spikes complements complex Multi-piece Charms (see page 123.)*

2 Lay the straight end of the wire on the steel block and hammer it flat with the ball-peen hammer.

Fish Charm

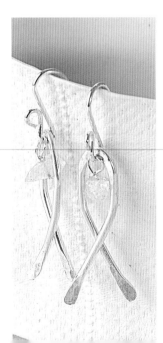

Left: *Such a simple yet evocative charm, which will hang happily with an ear wire or jump ring slipped through its "nose." Here, tiny stones hang within the bodies (see Looped Top Charm, page 121.)*

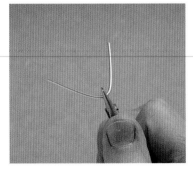

1 Cut 2½ in (6 cm) of 1.5 mm wire. File the ends smooth (see Filing Ends of Wire, page 96.) Grip the wire in the middle, close to the tips of round-nosed pliers, and bend the ends away from you.

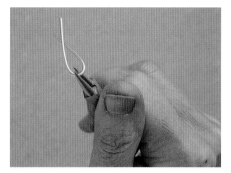

2 Continue bending the wire around the jaw, so that the ends cross over one another.

3 Lay the charm on the steel block and hammer the tail ends flat with the ball-peen hammer.

≈ Wire Heart Charm ≈

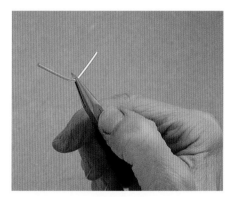

1 Cut 1¾ in (4.5 cm) of 1.5 mm wire. File the ends smooth (see Filing Ends of Wire, page 96.) Grip the wire just to one side of the middle with the tips of the jaws of chain-nosed pliers and bend one side up to make a "V" shape.

RIGHT: *Make the basic heart-shape a little more decorative still by curling the ends of the wire with round-nosed pliers before making the heart.*

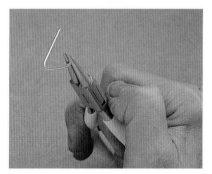

2 Hold one end of the wire with the tips of the jaws of round-nosed pliers. Bend the end in a curve to form one side of the top of the heart.

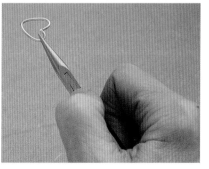

3 Bend the other end in the same way so that the ends touch. Hold one side of the top of the heart with chain-nosed pliers and adjust the join with your fingers so that the ends meet perfectly.

Wire Star Charm

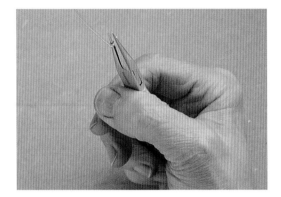

LEFT: *A classic charm shape that you can use to add meaning and visual interest to jewelry.*

1 Cut 1¾ in (4.5 cm) of 1.2 mm wire, File the ends smooth (see Filing Ends of Wire, page 96.) Grip one end of the wire close to the tips of the jaws of chain-nosed pliers and bend it to make a "V" shape.

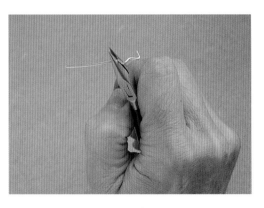

2 On the other side of the pliers, bend the wire in the opposite direction. Move the pliers to beyond the last bend and bend the wire again to make a zigzag shape.

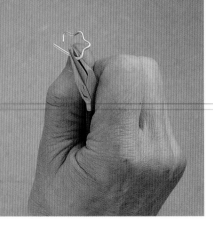

3 Continue bending to make five points, forming the wire into a circle with your hands as you work.

4 Hold the star close to one end with the pliers and push the ends together with your fingers so that they meet perfectly.

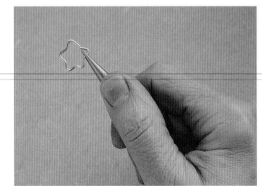

ᴧ Music Note Charm ᴧ

1 Cut 2⅝ in (6.5 cm) of 1.2 mm wire. File the ends smooth (see Filing Ends of Wire, page 96.) Grip one end of the wire close to the tips of the jaws of round-nosed pliers and start to form a coil.

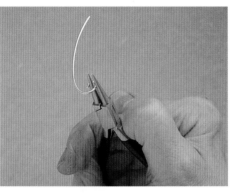

RIGHT: *A perfect charm to put on a piece for any music lover, whether they are a pop fan or a classical aficionado. Hang it with a jump ring through the top loop.*

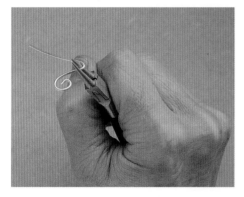

2 Hold the wire close to the tips of round-nosed pliers, ½ in (1 cm) above the coil. Bend the straight end of the wire back on itself.

3 Bend the wire right around to make a loop. Slip the straight end through the first coil, as shown.

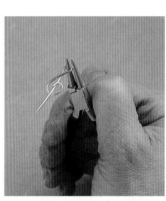

4 Using the tips of the jaws of round-nosed pliers, bend the end of the wire to form a small loop

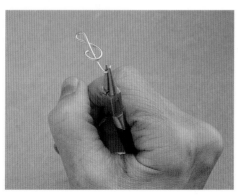

5 Lay the charm on the steel block and hammer the bottom loop flat with the ball-peen hammer.

Sheet Silver Charms

Solid silver charms in simple shapes will add weight and texture to your charm jewelry. Classic shapes are shown here, but you can experiment with your own motifs.

⇒ Heart Charm ⇒

1 Using a scriber, draw a heart shape onto a piece of sheet silver. Draw a freehand heart, or copy a template (see page 127.)

ABOVE: *A classic heart charm, which will find a home on any bracelet or necklace destined for family or dear friends.*

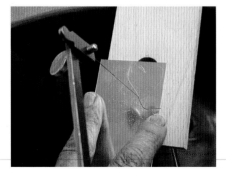

2 Use the file to make a notch where you want to start sawing. Using the fretsaw, cut out the heart (see Sawing Sheet Silver, page 97.) Cut up one side, then up the other side, and around the top.

3 Using the flat file and the polishing block, smooth the edges of the heart (see Filing, page 97 and Polishing, page 97.) Drill a hole to hang the charm from (see Drilling a Charm, page 118.)

Star Charm

1 Using a scriber, draw a star shape onto a piece of sheet silver. Draw a freehand star, or copy one of the templates (see page 127.) Use the file to make a notch where you want to start sawing. Using the fretsaw, carefully cut out the star. Cut into each notch in turn. Follow Step 3 of Heart Charm (see opposite) to finish the star.

ABOVE: *A shining star that will twinkle in your jewelry.*

Flower Charm

LEFT: *This is a pretty, naïve flower that will look sweet among other charms. Here, the silver has been hammered to add texture (see Hammering, page 120.)*

1 Using a scriber, draw a flower shape onto a piece of sheet silver. Draw a freehand flower, or copy one of the templates (see page 127.) Use the file to make a notch where you want to start sawing. Using the fretsaw, carefully cut out the flower. Cut out each petal in turn. Follow Step 3 of Heart Charm (see opposite) to finish the flower.

Disc Charm

RIGHT: *It is, of course, possible to draw and cut out your own discs, but it is difficult to make them perfectly circular. Instead, buy ready-made discs, which are available both drilled, and undrilled. The undrilled type tends to the thicker and works better for texturing or shaping. This disc has been textured with fabric (see Using Fabrics, opposite.)*

Drilling a Charm

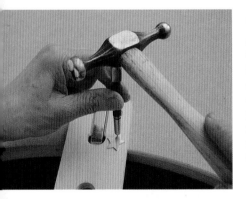

1 Position the tip of the center punch where you want to drill the hole. Sharply hit the other end of the punch with the flat central section of the ball-peen hammer head to mark the metal. You can use a small clamp to hold the charm still if you wish.

RIGHT: *Drill all your sheet silver charms in this way, then slip a jump ring through the hole to attach them to chain.*

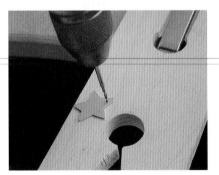

2 Place the bit of the hand drill on the marked point. Keeping the drill bit at right angles to the metal and pressing down gently, turn the handle slowly to drill the hole.

3 Push the point of the round file into the hole and twist it to file the edges of the hole smooth.

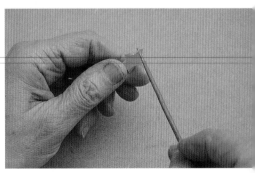

Texturing & Shaping

You can add texture to the surface of a sheet silver charm in one of two ways,
or gently curve it to make it three-dimensional.

~ Using Fabrics ~

1 Lay the fabric on the steel block and place the silver charm on top. Fold the fabric over it.

2 Using the flat-ended hammer, hammer the metal hard to transfer an impression of the fabric weave onto it..

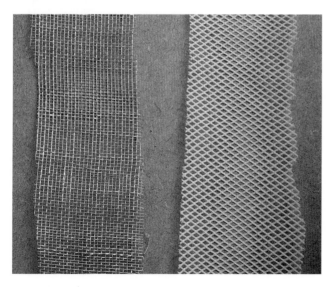

LEFT: *Experiment with different fabrics; those with a pronounced, open weave, like the ones shown here, will usually work best.*

RIGHT: *The texture makes light bounce off the silver, creating an attractive sparkle.*

Hammering

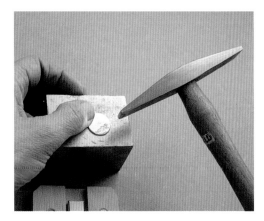

1 Lay the silver charm on a steel block. Use a short, sharp hammering action and keep the weight of the strokes consistent to produce an even texture. The corking hammer produces a series of short lines on the surface of the silver.

2 The ball-peen hammer produces a dimpled surface on the metal.

ABOVE: *The disc on the right is textured with the corking hammer and the one on the left with the ball-peen hammer.*

Doming

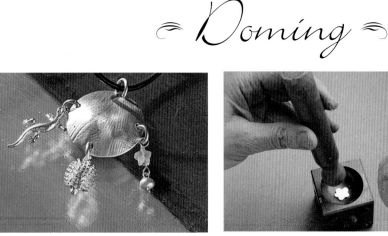

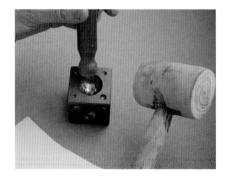

ABOVE: *Here, a large curved disc is the centerpoint of a necklace and has been drilled to hold three smaller charms.*

1 Lay the shape in the largest hole of the doming block. Place the rounded end of the wooden punch in the middle of the shape and hold the punch upright. Strike the other end of the punch firmly several times with the mallet.

2 Put the shape into the next hole down in size and repeat the process. Keep moving the shape to smaller holes until you have the degree of curve you want.

Threaded Charms

These charms are composed of different pearls and semi-precious stones and are almost limitless in their variety. Shown here are the simple techniques for creating them, but the finished charms can be as intricate as you wish.

ABOVE: *This is the simplest style of threaded charm.*

Looped Top Charm

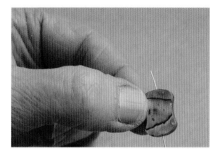 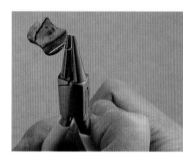 

1 Thread a bead onto a 0.5 mm wire and create a headpin. Here, a simple headpin is used (see page 105), but you can use a curly headpin (see page 105), or a zigzag headpin.

2 On the other side grip the wire close to the tips of the jaws of round-nosed pliers, just above the bead. Bend the wire around one of the jaws and then across itself.

3 Hold the wire loop with flat-nosed pliers and grip the end of the wire with the tips of the jaws of chain-nosed pliers. Use the chain-nosed pliers to tightly wrap the end of the wire several times around the base of the loop. Cut off any excess with wire cutters.

LEFT: *Any drilled stone, pearl, or bead can be made into a looped top charm; experiment with different elements and enjoy the results.*

LEFT: *You can make two or more elements into a single charm, but you may need to make a longer headpin (see Simple Headpin, page 105) to hold them.*

121

Looped Top & Bottom Charm

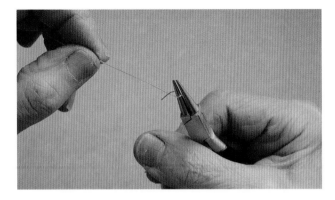

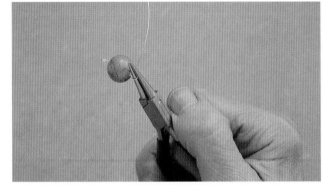

1 Grip a length of 0.5 mm wire close to the tips of round-nosed pliers, ⅝ in (1.5 cm) from one end. Follow Steps 2–3 of Looped Top Charm (see page 121) to make a wrapped loop.

2 Thread on bead and push it down to sit above the loop. Follow Steps 2–3 of Looped Top Charm to complete.

ABOVE: *This style of charm is a component of a multi-piece charm (see opposite.)*

ABOVE: *The central and top charms of these dangling earrings are looped top and bottom charms.*

LEFT: *Here, several looped top charms (see page 121) are threaded onto the bottom loops of looped top and bottom charms to create the clustered elements on these earrings.*

❧ *Multi-piece Charm* ❧

LEFT: *These Multi-piece Charms are so effective and can be made of as many elements as is practical for your piece of jewelry.*

ABOVE: *Try combining different sorts of stones and pearls, of varying sizes and shapes, in multi-piece charms to create original and striking charms.*

LEFT: *A multi-piece charm can be composed of silver charms as well as stones and pearls. Here, a looped top charm (see page 121) is threaded onto a curl charm (see page 110), which is attached to a textured disc (see Hammering, page 120, and Disc Charm, page 118) with a jump ring (see page 104.)*

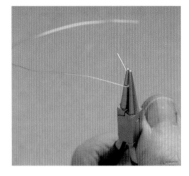

1 Grip a length of 0.5 mm wire close to the tips of the jaws of round-nosed pliers and bend it to make a "V" shape.

2 Thread on a looped top charm (see page 121.)

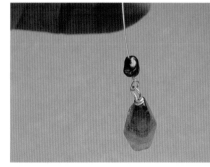

3 Follow Steps 2–3 of Looped Top Charm to make a wrapped loop.

4 Thread on the next element and make another loop. Repeat Steps 1–3, threading on the top loop of the charm, until you have added as many elements as you wish.

Wrapped Stone Charm

RIGHT: *This is the way to turn a stone you cannot drill into a charm.*

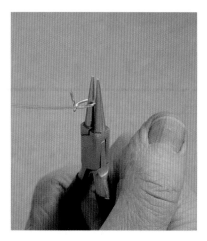

1 Cut a length of 0.8 mm wire: the precise length depends on the size of the stone, but cut a longer piece than you think you will need to be on the safe side. File the ends smooth (see Filing Ends of Wire, page 96.) Follow Steps 2–3 of Looped Top Charm (see page 121) to make a wrapped loop.

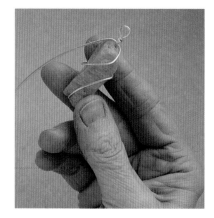

2 Position the loop at the top of the stone and just wrap the wire around it. Follow the natural shape of the stone and make the wrapping as simple or complex as you wish.

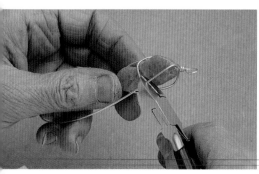

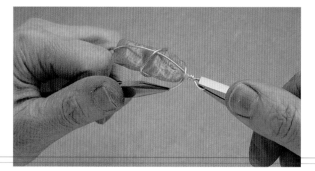

4 Hold the loop with flat-nosed pliers and grip the end of the wire with chain-nosed pliers. Use the chain-nosed pliers to tightly wrap the end of the wire several times around the base of the loop.

3 At the top of the stone, cut off any excess wire with wire cutters, but leave a ½ in (1 cm) tail.

LEFT: *This flat, carved shell flower has been wrapped to make a focal point for a necklace.*

Attaching Charms

Once you have made your charms you need to attach them to a chain to make a bracelet or necklace.
This can be done in one of two ways.

⇒ Attaching Charms Directly ⇐

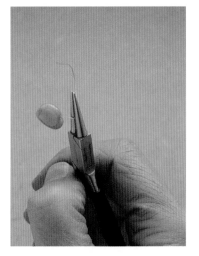

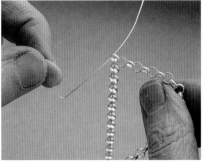

2 Thread the end of the wire through a link in the chain, where you want the charm to hang.

3 Grip the wire with the tips of the jaws of round-nosed pliers, just beyond the link. Hold the end with your free hand and wrap it tightly around itself, just above the bead, to make a wrapped loop. Cut off any excess wire with wire cutters.

1 Make a long headpin (see Simple Headpin, page 105.) Thread on a bead. Grip the wire close to the tips of the jaws of round-nosed pliers, just above the bead. Bend the wire to make a "V" shape.

LEFT: *Attaching a charm using this technique holds it close to the chain, giving a chunky look.*

Attaching Charms & Clasps
~ with Jump Rings ~

1 Hold one side of a jump ring with flat-nosed pliers. Slip on the charm and then the appropriate link of the chain.

2 Following Step 2 of Jump Rings (see page 104), close the ring.

LEFT: *This technique allows charms to dangle freely from the chain, giving more movement to the jewelry.*

RIGHT: *The same technique is used to attach a clasp, whether it be purchased or handmade, to the end of a length of chain.*

Templates

HEART
Heart Charm, page 116.

HEART
Heart Charm, page 116.

STAR
Star Charm, page 117

STAR
Star Charm, page 117

FLOWER
Flower Charm, page 117

FLOWER
Flower Charm, page 117

BOOKMARK
Bead Bookmark,
page 63

Index

Acknowledgments

Thanks to Cindy Richards who had faith in me, to Kate Haxell who gave me confidence and much support and to Tino Tedaldi for his patience.

Suppliers

Bellore
39 Greville Street
London EC1N 8P
Tel: 020 7404 3220
www.bellore.co.uk

Cookson & Exchange Findings
49 Hatton Garden
London EC1N 8YS
Tel: 020 7400 6500
www.cooksongold.com

Thunderbird Supply
1907 West Historic Route 66
Gallup, NM 87301
800-545-7968
www.thunderbirdsupply.com
Beads, findings, gemstones, tools

Phoenix Beads, Jewelry and Parts
5 West 37th Street
New York, NY 10018
212-278-8688
www.phoenixbeads.com
Imported glass, gemstone, pearl and crystal beads